FLUFF MY PILLOW, BEND MY STRAW

THE EVOLUTION AND UNDOING OF A NURSE

by

Joan Brady, RN, BSN

Edited by Mary Lou Diecker

Cover Design by Thomas Taylor of Thomcatt Graphics

VISTA PUBLISHING, INC.
473 Broadway
Long Branch, New Jersey 07740
(908) 229-6500

This publication is designed for the reading pleasure of the general public. All characters, places and situations are fictional and are in no way intended to depict actual people, places or situations.

Printed and bound in the United States of America on acid-free paper

ISBN: 1-880254-02-6
Library of Congress Catalog Card Number 92-061477

U.S.A. Price	$14.95
Canada Price	$21.95

DEDICATION

To my family, without whose constant and unwavering love I could not have survived

To Greg, Tommy and Matt, who made all the hard work, night shifts, weekends, etc., worth it

To Nancy, my friend, my advisor, and my "Cosmic Sister"

To Joseph Wambaugh, my inspiration

And . . . To Sister Mary Michael because, perhaps, it is time to forgive

PROLOGUE

Sister Mary Michael looked like a witch. She wore the kind of rimless, round spectacles you would expect to find on a witch or on a Sister of Charity in 1950.

Like any self-respecting witch, she also wore an all black habit that draped her shapeless nun's body. The only adornment on the whole outfit was a white, organdy headpiece which framed her withered old face and left little red marks in the parched, unyielding skin. Many of her first grade students deduced that the reason Sister didn't smile very much was because it must hurt to have that thing poking your face all day.

Sister said she had eyes in the back of her head and, if she said so, then thirty-eight first graders believed her. After all, anyone who dressed like a witch and claimed to be married to God, probably wouldn't lie.

A long black strand of rosary beads hung from somewhere on the mysterious attire. It served as a source of strength and serenity for Sister. Any time she felt herself running out of patience with her thirty-eight first graders, she had only to clasp the big silver and black crucifix in the palm of her hand, and she could actually feel Our Lord infusing her with strength.

Her first graders liked the rosary beads too - but not for the same reason. They liked the way the old wooden beads rattled together when Sister walked, warning them of her impending arrival whenever they had been left on their "honor" to behave and to be quiet.

On this particular multicolored, Autumn day, ears almost visibly perked up as the children heard the distant rattle of Sister's rosary beads. They settled down in plenty of time to convince Sister that they had all been perfect little angels while she had been gone.

"Today, children," Sister began before she even got through the doorway, "we are going to learn a Prayer for Vocations. Can anyone tell me what I mean by that?"

An eager hand in the back of the room shot up, followed by two more equally zealous ones in the front. Then it began to sound as if one of the old steam pipes had burst again.

"S-s-s-s."

Sister's trained ear recognized it as the sound of each child competing for her permission to blurt out the correct answer. After thirty-five years in the classroom, Sister Mary Michael knew that this odd "S" sound the children were making was short for "Sister Mary Michael," her hard-earned, precious and meaningful appellation. Such unbridled enthusiasm. Such disrespect. The children who knew the answer were practically falling out of their seats to be recognized. The children who didn't, were busy becoming invisible behind the person in front of them or suddenly becoming very interested in reading the catechism which lay open before them on their desks.

Sister could see that this was going to be a particularly tough group to tame. But if anyone could quell the spark and spunk of youth, Sister Mary Michael was the one to do it. In fact, many a former student looked back (usually from a psychiatrist's couch) and thought that Sister would have made an excellent lion tamer. Any circus or zoo would have been lucky to get her. Any first grade would have been lucky to get the Wicked Witch of the East **instead** of her.

One of the children trying to become invisible at this point was a quiet little girl in the third row named Courtney Quinn. Sister did not particularly like this child. Maybe it was because Courtney seemed too independent for a six-year-old - especially a six-year-old **girl.** Or maybe it was because she never seemed quite as intimidated as the other children when Sister told the class stories of the shrewdness of Satan. One thing that definitely annoyed Sister was the child's name. What kind of Roman Catholic parents could not name their child after a saint? And whoever heard of Saint Courtney? Sister felt annoyed enough to pick on the child again, except that she had recently heard that one of Courtney's seven or eight siblings, her infant brother in fact, had recently died from something called Sudden Infant Death Syndrome. Since then Courtney had been withdrawn and heavyhearted. Sister decided to have mercy - at least for awhile.

Courtney Quinn was sitting at her desk wondering why there always had to be so many different kinds of prayers to learn. Rosaries, Acts of Contrition, Requiems. And now a Prayer for Vocations. Courtney couldn't help wondering if God really cared whether or not you got the words right. Why couldn't she just talk to God in her own way and ask for the things she needed? She remembered the week before Timmy died, they had learned a prayer called Special Intentions. Courtney couldn't wait to say her prayers that night and try it out. She had a very special intention in mind.

As she knelt beside her bed, hands folded and head bowed, she began just the way Sister had taught them.

"Dear God, I have a very Special Intention for which I implore your intervention." There. Even though she didn't know what words like "implore" and "intervention" meant, she was certain there must be some magic in them. Now came the best part. The part where she could put her request in her own words.

"Please, God, please let Sister Mary Michael have a heart attack and die before school tomorrow."

Her mother had called it a sacrilege and said that Courtney would have to tell it in confession. And Sister Mary Michael showed up for school the next day looking healthy as a horse. So much for Special Intentions.

So now, here was a new one. Vocations. Why did she have to be what **God** wanted her to be? Why couldn't she just be what **she** wanted to be? She supposed it was some kind of sin to think that way. She hoped it wasn't another sacrilege. Her baby brother Timmy had died shortly after the last sacrilege she had committed. She hoped with all her heart the two events weren't connected.

She would never forget the sights and sounds of that horrible night. Her mother's panicked screams and Timmy's lifeless, pale form in their father's strong arms. No detail escaped her six-year-old memory. Fingers flew to telephones and furniture was hurled out of the way. The front door exploded into big, tall men dressed alike in blue coveralls with orange writing across their backs and carrying mysterious equipment. It was as though someone had turned up the volume - everything was so loud. A big, muscular man gathered up Timmy in hands that looked like they'd held more footballs than babies. The big man blew little butterfly breaths into the unresponsive infant.

"C'mon, son, you can do it," he pleaded in a whisper.

Courtney looked across the room at her sisters sitting with hands folded neatly in their laps and the frightened eyes taking it all in. She crossed the room to sit with them and suddenly everything was quiet again. Courtney knew what that meant. She couldn't bear to look anymore. She didn't want to remember this. But it was too late. The die was cast and the blueprint for her life had been formed. Timmy's distress and helplessness had planted the first seeds of a deep need to nurture and protect the sick. Courtney knew at that moment exactly how she wanted to spend her life.

Sister Mary Michael's sarcastic voice pierced Courtney's thoughts.

"Are you planning to join us, Miss Quinn, or do you already have a vocation?"

Courtney's classmates had already lined up to go next door to church to say the prayer they'd just learned while Courtney had been lost in her thoughts. Embarrassed, she rose from her desk and proceeded to the end of the line.

Once inside the church, girls on one side, boys on the other, the children bowed their heads and solemnly repeated the prayer with Sister's guidance. In an effort to conform, Courtney bowed her head and mumbled the meaningless words in unison with her classmates. But conformity would never be one of her strong points. Not ever. She clasped her hands tightly at the end of the prayer and added silently,

4

"Please, God, please don't make me be a nun. I swear I'll do anything, **ANYTHING** else, just **please** don't make me be a nun."

God must have heard her prayer that day . . . and her promise, for He let her slide on the nun stuff. But the promise to do **ANYTHING** carried a steep price with it. He made her a nurse. And He made her pay.

CHAPTER ONE

"HOSPITAL LINGO"

Courtney Quinn's first year as a Registered Nurse was spent on a sixty-bed Medical/Surgical floor of one of Philadelphia's largest and busiest teaching hospitals. The term "teaching hospital" referred to the fact that this was a hospital where interns and residents did their training. Usually these hospitals also included teaching programs for any related medical field, such as Nursing, Radiology technicians, etc.

When Courtney entered the ward of 6-South her first Saturday morning, she heard the raspy voice of Charge Nurse Maggie Ruggles squawking into the telephone.

"I don't give a shit what your numbers are! I have two patients about to code, one possible emergency O.R., a floor full of G.O.R.K.s, and nothing but new graduates for staff! You **have** to send me some help!"

Courtney assumed Maggie was talking to the Staffing Supervisor, but couldn't believe that anyone would speak to their superiors with such disrespect. Courtney obviously didn't know Maggie Ruggles yet.

"Fine," continued Maggie after a short pause. "Fine. But we're only giving P.T.A. baths and don't come crying to me when the patients fill out their Patient Satisfaction forms and they all say their dogs get better treatment at the Vet!"

She slammed down the phone and looked up at her dumbfounded audience of two new graduate nurses, Courtney Quinn and Karen Beal. The two new nurses had just finished two weeks of hospital orientation and this was their first day on their own. It was a typically short-staffed Saturday that would have been dangerously understaffed even if Courtney and Karen were seasoned R.N.s like Maggie. Words could not describe how desperately understaffed 6-South was today.

Maggie Ruggles studied them for a moment, then grumbled, "Quinn, you take 660 to 665. Beal, you take 666 to 670. Relieve each other for lunch if either of you is lucky enough to **get** lunch. Oh, yeah, the I.V. Nurse is out sick today so you'll have to draw your own blood work."

The two new nurses exchanged frightened looks then turned on their newly polished heels and headed for the Conference Room to receive Change of Shift Report. The girls were beginning to understand better than ever why it was called a teaching hospital. They had a feeling they had a lot to learn.

By the sound of report, Maggie had assigned them patients who needed mostly custodial care - ten each. She obviously didn't trust them yet with anyone who was **really** sick. She assigned herself to the really sick ones. They naively wondered why they had each just spent four years in college.

"What are P.T.A. baths?" Courtney whispered to Karen.

"I haven't the foggiest," Karen replied.

Report was begun by an exhausted looking Night Nurse who clearly wanted to get this over with as quickly and efficiently as possible. The tone of her voice told them not to ask questions, to just listen and get to work.

"660 is a twenty-eight-year-old Hispanic male with a diagnosis of priapism."

Her voice was expressionless and, except for an order for ice water enemas, there was nothing unusual about her report. Except that Courtney had no idea what priapism was ... and she didn't dare ask the irritable night nurse. She wordlessly questioned Karen with her eyes, but Karen merely shrugged.

As soon as report was finished, Courtney pulled out her pocket Medical Dictionary and looked up priapism. A veiny hand closed the book just as Courtney located the term, and a familiar, raspy voice said,

7

"It's a hard-on that won't quit."

Courtney looked into the expressionless face of Maggie Ruggles. "The guy has a hard-on," she continued, "and nothing will make it go down. If it stays up much longer it could make him impotent. It's your job to get it down or get him ready for the Operating Room - whichever comes first. No pun intended."

Courtney was speechless. Maggie was relentless.

"It probably would've made more sense for an old broad like me to take him, but there are too many sick patients on the floor today who need a **REAL** nurse. Start with the enemas. If it doesn't come down, call Dr. Weiss and let him know. And for God's sake, keep him N.P.O. Do you know what that means?"

"Nothing by mouth." Courtney was glad that she could at least give one correct answer.

"Right. He'll probably end up going to the O.R. anyway and the F.L.E.A.S haven't written the N.P.O. order yet, but that doesn't mean we can't think ahead a little."

"F.L.E.A.S?" Courtney asked.

"Fucking Little Egotistical Assholes," Maggie impatiently replied. "The medical docs. That's what we call them. The patient was admitted to their service, so they write all the orders even though Urology is doing all the work. He'll have to be transferred to their service before he goes to the O.R."

"I see," Courtney said, afraid to say anything else. She had no idea what any of this meant.

Courtney entered room 660, her arms laden with enema equipment, and thought she was seeing a teepee in the bed of Jose Rodriguez. The patient looked first at the ominous looking equipment, then at Courtney's young, lovely face. Though he spoke no English, he suddenly knew the meaning of ambivalence. Not surprisingly, the ice water enemas yielded no results. As predicted, the patient ended up in the Operating Room which meant there was one less P.T.A. bath to do ... whatever that was.

Courtney was busy mixing the afternoon I.V. antibiotics and still giving "morning" baths to some of her patients at two p.m., when she heard a doctor's voice demand of Maggie Ruggles, "I have just one question. Is one of those new nurses taking care of Jose Rodriguez? That Quinn girl, maybe?"

Courtney's heart sank. Could she have done something wrong already? It was only her first day on her own and obviously she had screwed something up on the priapism patient.

She approached the surgeon and the team of interns and residents who surrounded him.

"Yes, Dr. Weiss. I'm taking care of Mr. Rodriguez. Is something wrong?" In her Catholic heart she felt like she was saying, "Bless me, Doctor, for I have sinned."

The surgeon tried to hide a smile. "Yes," he said with false sincerity, as Courtney stood contritely in front of the group, ready to take the criticism.

"He's got another hard-on," the surgeon grumbled.

Sudden coughing fits erupted from the group of interns and residents as they tried to suppress smirks and outright laughter.

"I don't understand," said Courtney, for about the millionth time that day.

"Well, we took the patient to the O.R. and, under general anesthesia and sterile conditions, we inserted needles into the major vessels of the penis and aspirated blood until it was flaccid again." Dr. Weiss explained the procedure, much to his credit, in purely medical terms. "But now it appears his penis is erect again," he continued.

9

"But what can you do?" Courtney asked earnestly. "You can't put him under general anesthesia twice in one day, can you?"

Dr. Weiss looked pensive. "No, we can't," he finally answered. "I'll tell you what we can do though."

Courtney was all ears.

"I want you to take a blood pressure cuff, wrap it around his penis and put it up to forty. Leave it on for twenty minutes, then go in, let the air out and leave it off for twenty minutes. Then on twenty minutes, off twenty minutes. If you see any results, call Dr. Warren, my Chief Resident, and let him know."

"I don't understand. What will wrapping a blood pressure cuff around it do?" Courtney queried.

Dr. Weiss took an exaggerated moment to light his pipe. "Well," he said, "by applying even compression to the penis, perhaps we can force blood out through the opening we already made in the O.R. today, thereby saving the patient another surgery."

This made some kind of mechanical sense to Courtney and she certainly wasn't confident or experienced enough to question the decision of a doctor. The interns and residents all seemed to have some kind of coughing fit again as Courtney left the group to go find a sphygmomanometer. As she walked she thought about how much precious time this meant she was going to have to spend with this one patient. What about the other nine? They deserved her time and attention, too. She guessed this was what being a nurse was all about - establishing priorities and organizing your time.

When she entered the patient's room, his sleepy eyes recognized the blood pressure machine she wheeled in with her. Despite the language barrier, he pulled one arm from under the covers and extended it, figuring he knew what she wanted.

"No, no. no," she murmured.

Jose Rodriguez's eyes grew into saucers as Courtney, mustering all the professionalism she was capable of, whipped down the sheets and wrapped the blood pressure cuff around her patient's erect penis. She pumped the cuff up to 40 mm/Hg as instructed, then covered the whole hodgepodge with a sheet. Twenty minutes later, she returned to an anxious but delighted patient and let the air out of the cuff.

She repeated this process three or four times before Maggie Ruggles happened to walk into the room just as Courtney was pumping the cuff up to forty and Jose's brown eyes were rolling upward in thanksgiving for these wonderful American hospitals.

"What the f---?"

Courtney whirled around.

"Dr. Weiss told me this would help." It sounded weak.

"Are you fucking stupid, or what?"

Courtney was humiliated as she began to realize that she had been had. And the worst part was that this cynical, ruthless Maggie Ruggles character was going to point it out to her.

"I've seen some pretty naive new graduates in my time," Maggie laughed, "but you take the cake. This is great! A classic! Wait 'till everyone hears about this. Congratulations! How does it feel to hold the all time record for naiveté?!"

Maggie no longer looked tired or frustrated about the short staffing. In fact, she looked twenty years younger as she stood in the doorway laughing.

"O.K.," Courtney murmured. "I guess I've been a fool."

"I'll say!" Maggie roared mercilessly.

"Well, as long as I've been this stupid, I might as well show all of my ignorance. At least maybe I'll get something out of all this." She looked

11

at Maggie directly and continued. "I heard you talking on the phone this morning. You said you had a floor of G.O.R.K.s. What does that mean?"

Maggie didn't feel like answering questions. She wanted to just stand here for a few more moments laughing at this innocent and unjaded child. But she knew the question would eventually be answered and she may as well be the one to do it.

"G.O.R.K.?" she countered. "G.O.R.K. stands for 'God Only Really Knows.' When someone's all screwed up and no one, not even the F.L.E.A.s can really slap a diagnosis on them, then we say they're a G.O.R.K., or they're all G.O.R.K.ed out."

Courtney felt her stomach turn at the cynicism and detachment of this cold-hearted nurse. But she had never learned this kind of information in any of her college classes. She had taken a course in medical terminology, but that had mainly taught her pretty words like emesis, sputum and stool in place of lay language for puke, spit and shit. It hadn't been that difficult. But nowhere in those lists of words had there been anything like "G.O.R.K." or "F.L.E.A.s." or "P.T.A." baths.

"One more thing," she quickly added.

"Shoot."

"What's a P.T.A. bath?"

Maggie exploded into laughter again. "You mean you've been working all day with ten patients and didn't know what P.T.A. baths were?" She could see the answer to her questions in Courtney's expectant face. "It's a weekend bath," she said, "the kind we give when the floor is more short staffed than usual."

"What does it stand for?"

"Pits, Tits and Ass."

There was a whole new world out there that Courtney was going to have to learn her way around in and a whole new language in which she would have to become fluent if she were going to survive. She looked down at her blue and gold school pin and at the name tag with the cherished R.N. after it. . . and realized that had been the easy part.

CHAPTER TWO

"SOME ENCHANTED EVENING"

One of the first things a nurse learns to look for when she comes on duty is the presence of the crash cart. This is the cart where all the emergency equipment is kept in case a patient goes into cardiac or respiratory arrest. It holds all the necessary and life-saving drugs and paraphernalia to keep even the most lifeless heart pumping until the code team arrives, like bats out of hell, to try and save the day.

The presence of the cart in its usual central location on the ward reassures the oncoming nurse that at least there are no emergencies going on at the moment. Its absence means that there is chaos going on somewhere on the ward and that Change of Shift Report will be delayed, disjointed, and given by some very exhausted and probably irritable nurse who can't wait to go home. It is not a good way to start the shift.

The cart was missing when Courtney and Karen arrived to work their first 3 to ll shift. Since no one seemed to even notice their fifteen-minutes-early arrival, they decided to walk down the hall and see what all the excitement was about. The cart was in front of room 663 and there was a lot of shouting coming from the room.

"Are you getting a rhythm?" a doctor asked a nurse without taking his eyes off the lifeless form in the bed.

"Nothing," replied the nurse watching the flat line of the E.K.G. printout.

"Resume C.P.R.," the doctor ordered.

Two interns picked up where they had left off, one doing chest compressions while the other breathed rhythmically through the tube that had been inserted down the patient's throat.

Courtney and Karen stayed in the background, wanting to remain unnoticed, hoping to learn something. The room was at least ten degrees warmer than the rest of the ward and everyone on the team was sweating. The room looked like a ticker tape parade had just gone through. Everywhere there were strips of E.K.G. paper, caps from needles, extra syringes, wrappers from mysterious looking equipment and bags of I.V. fluids. Yet there was an orderliness to it. Poetry in motion at some points, as each member of the team concentrated on their own job and their own section of this person's body. The anesthesia resident was at the head of the bed "bagging" the patient with an ambu bag that forced air into the lungs through the tube he had just inserted through the mouth. The interns tirelessly continued C.P.R. Another resident was studying the E.K.G. printout which was now beginning to show some faint signs of life. A nurse was carefully drawing up medication in a syringe, while another nurse miraculously started an I.V. in an arm with a collapsed circulatory system.

Suddenly Courtney realized that the body they were working on was a woman. A human being. Probably someone's mother or sister or wife. She was amazed to realize how easily a person could become dehumanized in a situation like this. Yet, what choice did anyone really have? Just then one of the residents, who'd been "pushing" medications through one of the many I.V.s, came to stand in the empty space beside Courtney. He was sweating, yet calm and apparently unaffected by the urgency of the circumstances. He was tall and blonde and smiling as he leaned his back against the wall. He watched the continuing chaos around the bedside for a moment, then glanced down at Courtney, accurately interpreting the fear and inexperience that was written all over her face.

"Not a bad crowd for a Tuesday," he murmured without cracking a smile. But before Courtney could close her gaping mouth, the sharp finger of Maggie Ruggles was poking into her shoulder.

"Do you intend to get report some time today, Quinn? I would like to get out of here and go home, ya know."

The tall blonde resident turned to Maggie and said, "You mean you don't want to stay around and see what happens, Maggie?"

15

"I already know the ending. The patient dies, and you guys all walk out, leaving me with a mountain of paper work, a hysterical family to deal with and a room that looks like a tornado just swept through it."

"Ah, c'mon Mags, try not to get so emotional about it."

Courtney tried to suppress a smile, but nothing escaped the eye of Maggie Ruggles. She would have made a good nun.

"I don't know what you're smiling about, Quinn. When they get done making a mess up here, these guys are gonna go down to the Emergency Room and send you an admission. Just watch."

"Maggie, Admitting Office is on line four. They want to talk to you." The voice came from the intercom on the wall above the dying patient.

"Oh, Christ, what did I tell you," Maggie mumbled as she walked out the door.

"Don't let her fool you," quipped the blonde resident, "she's nuts about me."

Courtney took one last look at the shambles of the room and the body of the woman who was just trying to die. She signaled to Karen that they had better get out to the Conference Room and start report.

As they approached the Nurses' Station, they could hear the unmistakable voice of Maggie Ruggles shouting into the phone, "Jesus Christ! The bed isn't even cold yet! Give us a chance, will ya?"

A large group of doctors and nurses walked past the Nurses' Station at that moment, some engrossed in serious debate about the cause of death and others catching up on the news in one another's lives. The tall blonde doctor was the last to pass and he pounded a fist on the desk as he sauntered by and bellowed, "You were right, Mag Pie. Got any hunches on the horses?"

But Maggie was too busy arguing on the phone with the Admissions Office to pay him any mind.

16

"What do you think this is? A Maternity Ward?" she continued. She listened for a moment to the person on the other end of the line, then guffawed and added, "Yeah, right. I suppose you're gonna tell me now that I just happen to have the only empty female bed in the whole friggin' hospital. Well I've got a news flash for you. There's still a patient in that bed. A dead one, but a patient no less."

When the argument ended and Maggie hung up the phone, she informed the two young nurses that they were to call Admitting as soon as the body was removed and the room cleaned so that the Emergency Room could send them a threatened AB.

"Threatened Abortion?" Courtney said incredulously. "I don't know very much about Obstetrics."

"Well, get ready to learn. And maybe even go fishing tonight."

"Fishing?"

"Yeah. If she loses the pregnancy on your shift, she'll probably lose it on the toilet. They usually do. That means you'll have to put on rubber gloves and fish it out so you can send it to the Lab to be analyzed."

. . . . .

An hour later, twenty-three-year-old Mary Richards arrived on the ward via stretcher. She was accompanied by her handsome husband who held her hand as he walked along beside the stretcher. The patient was transferred onto a bed without ever letting go of her husband's hand. She was ten weeks into her much wanted first pregnancy, and had begun to have some spotty bleeding last night. Despite remaining on strict bedrest as ordered by her physician, the bleeding had increased and she was brought to the Emergency Room.

Courtney was instructed to check the amount of vaginal bleeding and the patient's vital signs at least once every hour, and to call the OB/GYN resident if there were any changes. Courtney's heart ached for the young couple as she noticed the husband sitting on the bed, reassuring his wife and picking out names for their future child.

The evening was a blur of patient call lights, ringing telephones, and piles of charts with stat orders on them. Courtney was just about to sit down and go over the charts for patients who were scheduled for surgery the next morning. All of these charts were expected to have signed consents and the results of recent blood and urine tests on them. Just as Courtney piled up a stack of seven charts to check, she noticed the call light blinking over the bathroom door of Mary Richards.

When Courtney reached the room, she gently knocked with one hand and opened the door with the other. Mary Richards was sitting on the toilet all bent over and crying softly.

"I think I lost it," she sobbed, looking up at Courtney.

"Do you think you can walk back to your bed if I help you?"

"Yes, I think so."

Gently, very gently, Courtney helped Mary to her feet. Mary stood, and both she and Courtney peered at the soft, bloody remains of Mary's desperately wanted pregnancy.

"That's it, isn't it?" Mary cried softly, "That's my baby."

Courtney's heart broke for her. "There's really no way to be sure yet," Courtney answered, trying to take away some of the girl's pain. "Let's get you into bed and I'll call the doctor." Courtney took a quick set of vital signs and was relieved to see that they were stable. She cleaned some of the blood off the patient's legs, covered her, and headed for the phone in the Nurses' Station.

The Ward Secretary listened to Courtney's conversation with the resident and watched Courtney as she donned a pair of rubber gloves and picked up a specimen cup.

"Goin' fishin', huh, Quinn?" she chuckled.

Wanda the Ward Clerk liked to see new nurses panic. She was cold and heartless and refused to do anything that was not in her job description. Courtney was not about to give her the satisfaction of seeing how uncomfortable this made her.

Courtney was in the Dirty Utility Room labelling the specimen cup with a tag that read nothing of how much Mary Richards had wanted this baby or how long she'd been trying to get pregnant or how her heart was breaking right now. Soft footsteps behind her brought Courtney back to the moment. She turned around and found herself looking into the blue eyes of the blonde resident from the code this afternoon.

"You look mighty deep in thought, Nurse," he remarked. "Thinking about what's in the specimen cup, aren't you?"

"How did you know that?" She was surprised by this sudden show of sensitivity.

"It's written all over your face," he laughed. "Besides, I used to do the same thing when I first started in this business. But if you want to survive, I'm afraid you're going to have to toughen up a little."

"I don't want to toughen up," she answered. "Not if it makes me anything like some of the people I've met around here."

He laughed softly at her, shaking his head. "You'll see," he said. "Working in a hospital is a lot like fighting a war. You just get up every morning, put on your fatigues, and go out and fight the war for one more day and hope to God that you can survive it."

"That's depressing."

"That's reality. Speaking of which, Ms. Richards is going to have to go to the O.R. tonight. I just examined her and she's going to need a Dusting and Cleaning, so keep her N.P.O."

"Dusting and Cleaning?"

"Yeah, you know, a D and C."

"Oh."

With that, this now familiar stranger was out the door. Courtney didn't even know his name, but she had a feeling she hadn't seen the last of him. She was right.

. . . . .

Mary Richards went to the O.R. and Courtney Quinn went back to checking the pre-op charts. It was ten-thirty by then. To her dismay, Courtney found three charts with no recent bloodwork on them. She presented the dilemma to Wanda the Ward Clerk, hoping for some sound advice.

"What?" she asked, astounded. "It's ten-thirty at night and **now** you tell me you ain't got no bloodwork on three people? Honey, you're up shit's creek without a paddle. The Lab won't do pre-operative bloodwork after eight o'clock. You're sunk. Those cases are all gonna have to be cancelled and it's gonna be all your fault. Those doctors are gonna be **pissed** and I can't say I blame them."

This was the last straw. Courtney wanted to cry, but she would walk barefoot over hot coals before she would let this witch of a Ward Clerk know it. She wondered if she spoke to the people in the Lab and explained the situation, perhaps they would understand and have pity on her, just this one time.

"Do you know what time it is?" barked the voice of the Lab Technician over the phone. "Nothin' doin'. We only do pre-op until eight o'clock."

"But the floor's been really busy and . . . ."

"Not my problem."

Click.

Courtney placed the receiver in its cradle and wondered out loud, "What's gonna happen now?"

"Three O.R.s will get cancelled and you'll probably get bawled out by three different surgeons," said Wanda the Ward Clerk matter-of-factly. "I wouldn't want to be in your shoes," she chuckled.

Just then the doors opened and an orderly pushing a gurney rolled past them. It was Mary Richards being brought back from her surgery. Courtney grabbed the sphygmomanometer and followed them down the corridor. She helped slide Mary onto the freshly made up bed and began taking her vital signs. Vital signs were stable and there was no more vaginal bleeding. Mary was sleeping peacefully, no trace of the underlying sadness on her pretty young face. Suddenly, Courtney envied her. What she wouldn't give to be lying comfortably in bed now and not have to face the wrath of those three surgeons who would have to be notified of their cancelled cases.

She walked slowly back to the Conference Room, picked up a stack of charts on the way and decided to put off dealing with the doctors until she got some of her Nurse's Notes written. But she couldn't keep her mind off the mess she had made of things. She put her pen down, then her head down and wallowed in her exhaustion and frustration.

Just as she had allowed a couple of pent-up tears to roll down her cheeks, she heard a soft male voice behind her.

"Excuse me, are you the Charge Nurse?"

"Not for much longer," Courtney answered, not caring how much harm she could do at this point. She lifted her teary face to see none

21

other than the same blonde, blue-eyed resident who kept popping up at the strangest moments.

"I think maybe it's about time we introduced ourselves," he laughed as he recognized her. "I'm Dave Strauss," he smiled, extending his hand. Courtney placed her hand in his and shook it.

"My name's Courtney Quinn."

"Well, Courtney Quinn, first of all, how is my patient, Mary Richards, doing? Did she get back here yet from the Recovery Room?"

"Yes, she got back about twenty minutes ago. Her vitals are O.K. and she's not having any bleeding. She's doing O.K."

"And how is her nurse doing?" he asked with a note of concern in his voice.

The kindness of his question touched off a torrent of emotions that had been struggling for release all evening.

"Her nurse isn't doing so hot. In fact, I guess I really screwed up pretty badly." Courtney couldn't stop herself from spilling her feelings and a few tears. "It's my first time on 3 to ll and they put me in charge, and so much went on that I ended up getting three patients cancelled for the O.R. tomorrow and now I have to call their doctors and let them yell at me, and I'll probably end up getting fired."

"Wait a minute. Back up," he laughed. "It can't be as bad as all that."

"Believe me, it is. I don't think I'll ever get used to this place. I've made a mess of everything."

David Strauss, M.D., looked at Courtney for a long moment. "Tell me," he said, his voice filled with admiration, "how did you manage to get three patients cancelled for the O.R.? I'd really like to know. That information could come in very handy someday when I have forty-eight hours' worth of surgery to do in twenty-four."

Courtney looked up at him, not knowing whether or not to take him seriously.

"Oh, come now," he smiled. His voice was gentle and he placed a thumb on one of her tears and brushed it away. Suddenly she felt safe. She sensed that this handsome blonde stranger was about to save the day. He placed two strong hands on her shoulders and continued, "Why don't you tell me what really happened, and we'll see if we can't think of a solution. It would be a shame to see such a pretty face on the unemployment line."

Courtney blurted out the whole story, including the way Wanda the Ward Clerk had seemed to take such delight in Courtney's predicament.

"I see. Sounds like you've really had a night of it." He was pensive for a moment, then added, "It's true that the Lab won't run bloodwork after eight o'clock, but they'll do it any time if it's ordered stat by the doctor."

Courtney felt a glimmer of hope. "Would you?" she asked, amazed at his kindness.

Without answering, he picked up the phone and dialed the Lab.

"Hi, Betsy? This is Dave Strauss. How are you? Where have you been? I haven't seen you since Mark Duffy's party."

Courtney could hear a female voice giggling on the other end of the line as this Dave character continued to flirt with her. It was the same cold shrew who had hung up on her earlier.

"Listen, Betsy, I'm up on 6-South and there are a couple of patients, three to be exact, who need some stat bloodwork done. Do you think you could run it for me tonight?"

Courtney could hear the voice that was now dripping with honey agree to run any bloodwork that "Dave" needed.

23

"Thanks, Betsy, you're a doll. I knew I could count on you. Listen, you take care now. I'll be in touch." Click.

Dave turned to Courtney. "Mission accomplished," he smiled.

Suddenly, Courtney was painfully aware of Dave's muscular arms and the dark chest hairs that peeked over the V-neck of his O.R. greens . . . and of her mascara-streaked face and watery eyes. Dave pulled a handkerchief from his back pocket, placed it over her nose and said "Blow."

Courtney blew her nose and wiped her eyes. "You saved my life tonight. Thank you."

"That's what all the girls say."

Courtney smiled. She was utterly charmed by this man.

"You're much prettier when you smile, Courtney Quinn."

Courtney's stomach picked that moment to grumble audibly.

"Sounds like someone didn't have time for dinner tonight," Dave observed. "Want to meet me for a bite to eat when you get off duty?"

"Isn't the cafeteria closed at this hour?"

"Leave the logistics to me. I'm an expert. How does shrimp salad sound?"

It sounded wonderful, but then, "shit on a shingle" would have sounded wonderful if it were shared with this man.

"It sound great."

"Good. I'm gonna go take a shower and change my clothes. I'll meet you down at the Information Desk in half an hour, O.K.?" And with that, he disappeared down the hall.

Courtney gathered up her charts to make some final notations in them and brought them out to the Nurses' Station just as Wanda the Ward Clerk was packing up to go home.

"So you met Dr. Dave," she said solicitously.

"Yes, I did." Courtney tried to sound unimpressed, but nothing could hide the sparkle in her eye and the spring in her step.

Wanda looked at her knowingly. "You may have slithered out of one problem tonight, honey, but you sure as hell have bought yourself a much bigger one if you get involved with that man."

"What's that supposed to mean?" Courtney asked a bit defensively.

Wanda the Ward Clerk just shook her head. "Dr. Dave can be very charming," she chuckled, "but if you fall for any of that charm, you'll live to regret it. I've watched it happen a thousand times before. And, honey, you've got the look already. Fasten your seat belt . . . you're in for a fall. You'll see."

It may have been the only time Courtney should have heeded Wanda the Ward Clerk's advice.

Courtney took off her white nurse's cap and pulled the pins out of her thick brown hair, letting it tumble to her shoulders. She took out her hairbrush and brushed all the way down six floors in the elevator. When the elevator doors opened in front of the Information Desk, her hair was smooth and shiny and her face was glowing. Dave was standing there waiting for her, just as he had said he would. He gave her an approving smile then asked, "Ready for an adventure?"

"I was expecting a shrimp salad," she laughed. "You didn't say anything about an adventure."

"Follow me," he grinned.

He took her down hallways she'd never seen before. There were no patient rooms here or bustling Nurses' Stations, just big, important

25

looking doors with names stenciled on them. The hallways were meticulously clean and frighteningly quiet. They passed a few old men from the Housekeeping Department who were sitting inside an office marked "Executive Director." The men were sitting in plush chairs with their feet propped up on an expensive looking oak table as their brooms and mops and pails rested against the mauve-colored walls. Dave laughed as he passed them, then backed up and stuck his head inside the office door.

"Don't forget to put in a little extra pay this week when you sign the checks, boss," Dave quipped.

This brought a roar of laughter from the housekeepers and the man sitting at the head of the table called after Dave, "You got it, Dr. Dave. How much do you want?"

The group laughed and Dave and Courtney continued their journey through this foreign part of the hospital. They turned a corner and Dave tapped lightly on an unmarked door.

"Hey, Lulu, it's me," he whispered. "You got something for me?"

A lock turned slowly from inside the door, and a middle-aged black woman, wearing a tattered housekeeper's uniform, opened the door slowly. Her face broke into an enormous smile when she saw Dave.

"Yeah, I knew you was on call tonight," she said through her smile. "I hope you really hungry, too, 'cause I saved you a lotta food. I'm glad to see you brung a friend wif you to help you eat it all." She shared her big smile with Courtney for a moment, then reached into a worn looking pocket and handed Dave a single gold key.

"Now, don't you forget where to leave the key for me," she said in a semi-scolding tone.

Dave grabbed her leathery hand before she could pull it back and kissed it.

"Oh, go on! Shoo!" she said, somewhat embarrassed, but obviously pleased with Dave's show of affection. Then she closed the door in their faces and they heard the cylinder roll over the lock again.

"Did you ever think about running for mayor?" Courtney asked.

Dave reached for Courtney's hand and led her expertly through the labyrinth of corridors. She felt a bit weak in the knees as she followed his lead. Maybe it was hunger. Or maybe she was just plain tired. Or maybe she just liked the feeling of someone so tall and strong and sure of himself guiding her through this unfamiliar and sometimes cruel hospital world.

Dave stopped suddenly and slid the gold key into a door marked "Conference." He stood back and allowed Courtney to enter first. Her eyes widened with awe at what she saw.

There was an enormous oak table in the middle of the room surrounded by at least thirty plush, overstuffed, mauve-colored chairs. Expensive looking oil paintings hung on the walls and the ceiling-to-floor windows were covered with mauve velvet drapes. An ornate, silver serving cart stood next to the table. It was covered with shrimp salad, sandwiches, cookies, coffee and milk.

Observing her awestruck reaction, Dave leaned back on the now closed door and said, "This, Miss Quinn, is how the other half lives."

"The other half of what?"

"Of us. They're the brown-nosers, the bullshit artists, the red tape producers, the bureaucracy. But, for short, we call them Administration."

"Wow!" was all Courtney could utter. The room was magnificent. And the food didn't look bad either. Suddenly she was ravenous.

"What's your pleasure, Madam?" Dave asked, as he pulled out a chair at the head of the table for her.

"I don't suppose you'd have any shrimp salad," she asked, playing along with him.

"But of course, Madame. Anything your heart desires . . . as long as it's shrimp salad and chocolate chip cookies."

He took the seat next to her and they each wolfed down a big thick sandwich and a few chocolate chip cookies. Feeling stuffed and relaxed, Courtney leaned back in her chair and put her tired, battered feet up on the chair next to her, while Dave started in on another sandwich.

"I think I'm in the wrong field," Courtney mused as she looked around the room. "Maybe I should pursue Administration."

"We're both in the wrong field," Dave managed to mumble around chunks of shrimp.

"What do you mean by that?" Courtney was surprised.

"I mean you and me, nurses and doctors. We're on the caring end of things. That's the end where you work your tail off and no one ever says 'thank you.' Especially your employers - the pot-bellied guys who sit around in rooms like this all day making decisions that make life rough for you and me and the patients."

"Why is everyone in this place so jaded and angry?" Courtney asked.

Dave smiled shortly at this incredibly idealistic and naive creature in front of him. "Don't you see, Quinn? Hospitals are businesses and they capitalize on innocent, young, trusting nurses like you and eager young doctors like me who will work short-staffed and do double shifts for less than what a grocery clerk makes. They'll use you 'til you lie down and cry 'Uncle' and have nothing left to give. You begin to hate everybody and start seeing the patient as some unfortunate slob who's at the mercy of the system. You start to divorce yourself from any kind of emotion or it will kill you. You start making crude jokes 'cause if you don't, you'll die. It has to be that way. You know the type. There's a nurse on your floor like that - Maggie Ruggles."

"Oh, please. Don't tell me I'm going to eventually turn out to be another Maggie Ruggles."

"You better hope you do. She's a terrific nurse. And believe it or not, she's got a heart of gold."

"I don't believe it."

"You've got a lot to learn, Courtney Quinn."

"Maybe so. But I didn't become a nurse so that I could order people around like some kind of arrogant, unemotional robot."

"Maybe not. And maybe you won't get like her. But you'll eventually have to find your own way to cope. Maggie's a great nurse and I know I always feel better when I have a really sick patient on your floor if Maggie is on duty."

Courtney had never heard a doctor speak respectfully of a nurse before. She was astounded. Especially since the nurse was Maggie Ruggles. Maybe she had judged too quickly. Maybe she should watch Maggie more closely.

"Why are we talking shop?" Dave said, noticing the pensive look on Courtney's face. "Let's talk about something else."

"Like what?"

Dave thought for a moment. "Like the rumor I heard about you."

"Rumor? About me?" Courtney didn't know whether to be flattered or upset. She was mostly flattered that she was important enough to be talked about. She couldn't imagine what he could possibly be referring to.

Dave was evasive. He enjoyed teasing her. "Well, of course I'm not saying it's true, but I heard that you have an ardent admirer."

"I do? Really? Who?" She studied his blue, blue eyes, searching for a clue and hoping that he would say that it was a certain OB/GYN resident. He looked so appealing and boyish as he sat there munching on cookies and licking off the milk mustache.

29

"A wild Latin type. I think they said his name is Jose Rodriguez."

It took a moment to sink in, and then she remembered. The priapism man. "Oh no!" Her face felt like it was on fire "How did you hear about that?"

Dave broke into a fit of laughter. He threw his head back and held his sides. "I can't believe you really did that. That's the greatest story I've heard in a long time."

Courtney was appalled. Here she was, wildly attracted to this man and already he knew her deepest, darkest secret. She was mortified.

"You know you're famous throughout the hospital, don't you?" He kept laughing. His face was beautiful when he laughed. "Did you **really** wrap a blood pressure cuff around his dick?"

Courtney leaned forward to put her hand over his mouth, but he leaned farther back. She didn't want to hear the embarrassing words. She leaned farther forward and before she knew it, they were both in slow motion as Dave's chair tipped over backward and they tumbled to the floor together laughing.

Courtney landed on top of him as he let his head fall backward onto the thick mauve carpet.

"Are you hurt?" she asked, always the nurse, suddenly aware of the hair on his chest again.

"Do I look hurt?" he asked breathlessly through his laugher. "I haven't felt this good in a very long time."

"It's really not funny, you know," Courtney said, trying to sound a little offended.

"I think it's hilarious." His eyes sparkled with laughter in his flushed face.

Courtney rolled off of him and lay beside him on the plush carpet. Was it possible that only a few short hours ago she had been feeling so overwhelmed and frustrated? She propped her head on her hand and studied him.

He lay there for a moment, staring into space and scratching his belly, lost in his thoughts. Then, with a sudden burst of energy, he was in a standing position, towering over Courtney and extending his hand to help her up. She hesitated for a moment, then placed her hand in his. For one lovely moment, she felt small and helpless and he seemed so wonderfully strong and protective. He pulled her to her feet and she was only inches from his face. A face with curved lines around the mouth . . . evidence of thousands of preceding smiles. Suddenly it was hard to breathe.

"I guess I'd better be going," she said breathlessly.

"Yeah, I guess so," he said, never batting an eye.

And just as she was about to make a clean break - really she was - his boyish mouth closed in on her. On some distant level, she knew she was a goner.

CHAPTER THREE

"TOMMY"

Tommy Matthews was a patient who had a bad disease and a bad reputation. When the nurses gave Change of Shift Report on him, it was impossible not to notice the frustration in their voices. Tommy had Leukemia and this was his eighth admission to the hospital in the last two years. He was fifteen years old. He was too old for the Pediatric floor but far too young to be treated like an adult with a terminal illness.

"644 is Tommy Matthews, fifteen years old, for Dr. Shapiro, with Leukemia." Report always began professionally enough, but inevitably deteriorated into frustrated opinions, no matter who was reporting. Today it was a Float Nurse, someone who normally worked on another floor in another specialty, but who was pulled to 6-South because of extremely short staffing. Whenever someone got pulled to 6-South, they could plan on getting Tommy Matthews for a patient. The regular nurses on 6-South were sick and tired of him and took turns caring for him. No one could take him for more than one day at a time.

The nurse continued her report. "King Tommy is on a Regular Diet, but won't eat a thing. I medicated him for pain three times today and already he's asking for more." She sounded disgusted. "He's not due for an injection again 'til four o'clock, but hold him off as long as you can. He's really taking an awful lot of Demerol."

Courtney Quinn didn't understand what was so terrible about a sick and uncomfortable patient taking pain medication but, then, there was a lot she didn't understand, so she kept her mouth shut and listened as the nurse droned on.

"He refused his bed bath this morning and wouldn't let me change his bed. This kid can be really stubborn. If he asks to have his bed changed on your time, I hope you tell him to take a hike. He needs to realize he's **not** some kind of king around here."

When report finished, the Staffing Office called and said someone from 6-South had to be floated to Maternity. Karen Beal was next on the list of names of people whose turn it was to float. She looked terrified. The only words of comfort Courtney could offer were, "Maybe you won't have to go fishing."

This left Courtney in charge, since she and Karen were the only R.N.s on the 3 to 11 shift, and now Karen was leaving. Courtney didn't know whose shoes she'd rather be in.

Courtney always began her shift by making rounds on all of her patients, trying to put faces to the log of clinical information she received in report. Besides, sometimes this would be the only time during her shift that she would actually see some of the patients. It was an extremely busy and understaffed floor and it was usually the old story of only the squeaky wheels getting the oil. She walked into room 644 expecting to find a monster named Tommy. What she actually found was a fifteen-year-old boy sitting on his bed wearing a Pirates baseball cap and reading an Incredible Hulk comic book.

"Hi!" she said brightly.

He returned her greeting with a non-committal "hi," which he muttered without ever taking his eyes off his comic book.

"My name is Courtney," she continued, undaunted. "I'm the Charge Nurse tonight . . . so . . . if you need anything, give me a call, O.K.?"

He put the comic book down and looked up at her with big brown eyes. "My name is Tommy," he said.

"I know," Courtney smiled. "And I see you're an Incredible Hulk fan," she added, trying to maintain this unexpected line of communication they'd suddenly established.

"How come you're trying to be nice to me?" he asked with all the honesty of a terminally ill child. "Didn't the day shift nurses tell ya what a pain in the ass I am?" he challenged.

33

"I . . . well . . . I . . . "He'd caught her off guard and he knew it. He enjoyed watching her struggle to regain her composure.

"They told me you didn't want your sheets changed," she said, trying very hard to sound non-judgmental.

But Tommy was not through with her. He was going to test her . . . her patience and, more importantly, her honesty. "Ah, c'mon. I been comin' to this floor now for two years. I know the nurses all sit down at three o'clock and talk about us patients. I'm sure they told ya what a pain in the ass I was that I didn't eat or take a bath or let them change my sheets. I bet they even told you not to give me anymore Demerol shots," he said knowingly.

"Are you having a lot of pain today, Tommy?" she asked earnestly.

"Nah." There was the slightest hint of macho pride in his voice.

"So how come the shots?" She could be forthright too.

"I just feel like it, that's all. It gets boring around here, ya know. And when I get the shots, I don't mind the boredom so much."

"I see," said Courtney in a pensive tone. "I guess I'd be bored, too, if I had to hang around here twenty-four hours a day."

Tommy couldn't believe his ears. Was it possible that somebody actually understood?

"What else do you think would keep you from being bored?" Courtney added with genuine concern.

"Sometimes I play my guitar." He said it almost shyly.

Courtney spotted the guitar leaning against the wall at the foot of his bed.

"Do you think you could play a song for me? I love the guitar." She was thinking of how much work she had waiting for her outside the door.

But this seemed terribly important.

The rebellious look on his face softened to that of a vulnerable little boy. He picked up his guitar and strummed a soft, Bob Dylan-ish sound.

"Do you sing?" she asked.

"I thought you'd never ask," he grinned. And with that he broke into a boyish rendition of Bob Dylan's "Rolling Stone."

Courtney applauded and Tommy blushed. "That was great, Tommy! Will you do another for me later if I can get a few free minutes?"

"I'm not going anywhere." There was sadness in his voice.

"O.K., I'll be back," Courtney promised. "I gotta run. I've got a million things to do out there. But I have a feeling this will have been the best part of my night. Thank you, Tommy."

Courtney finished her rounds and returned to the Nurses' Station to find a Nurse's Aide cupping her hand over an elderly old man's ear and yelling into it, "I need a sputum specimen." The old man had no idea what she was talking about as she shouted and pointed to the cup she was trying to hand him.

"Huh? What?" was all the old man could say. He had just been admitted for gall bladder surgery in the morning, and his doctor ordered several specimens for cultures to be collected on him since he'd been running a low grade fever.

"Let me try," said Courtney to the frustrated Nurse's Aide. "Mr. Carson, we need a specimen. We need you to spit in the cup," she shouted. The old man put his hand to his ear and repeated "Huh? What?"

"SPIT IN THE CUP!" Courtney and the Aide shouted in unison.

"Oh, oh, all right," the man said disgustedly and walked off down the hall carrying the treasured specimen cup.

Courtney had all but forgotten about the needed sputum specimen within the next five minutes, since phones rang continually and busy interns and residents filled the Nurses' Station. Admitting called and said they were sending a twenty-six-year-old patient with Lupus Erythematosis and where would she like to put "it." Courtney was tempted to tell them "On another floor," but then quickly realized that was the kind of response Maggie Ruggles would have given. She decided to put the patient in 644 with Tommy. They were both young and maybe they would get along well. Up until now, everyone had been afraid to give Tommy a roommate because of his ornery moods. Courtney thought a roommate might be just what Tommy needed.

The new admission's name was Michael McClendon. He was young and handsome and surprisingly healthy looking for someone with a serious disease. Then she remembered that these patients were known for a pinkish "butterfly" rash over the face which, at first glance gives them the appearance of glowing good health. To the untrained eye, there is no obvious evidence that a deadly disease of the connective tissue is going on beneath the healthy looking exterior. Courtney liked Michael. He was pleasant and friendly and a perfect roommate for Tommy.

As Courtney headed for the Nurses' Station after admitting Michael McClendon, she saw Mr. Carson standing at the desk, wearing only a patient gown with no underwear. The back of the gown was open and Mr. Carson's eighty-year-old buttocks were exposed as he stood there unintentionally mooning unsuspecting visitors.

As Courtney got closer, Mr. Carson shoved a specimen cup at her containing an enormous piece of stool and said grumpily, "Here. Is this what you want?"

Courtney was taken aback for a minute, especially as horrified visitors looked from his backside to the cup he was holding and waited to see what Courtney was going to do.

"No, no, Mr. Carson, I said **SPIT** in the cup."

The old man disgustedly took his specimen as though it had been some kind of precious gift and walked toward his room, shaking his head and mumbling something about "Why can't people make up their minds around here."

Just then Wanda the Ward Clerk informed Courtney that the Nursing Supervisor was on the phone and wanted to speak to the Charge Nurse immediately. Courtney took the phone.

"This is Miss Quinn speaking."

"Quinn, this is Mrs. Cassidy in the Nursing Office. I was wondering if you could do us a big favor and work a double shift tonight. We're really short staffed and we have no one to cover your floor on nights. Would you be a doll and help us out?"

Courtney didn't see any reason not to. Besides, she was glad that they obviously trusted her enough to run the floor by herself for two shifts. Naively, she was sort of flattered.

"Sure, I'll do it," she answered.

"Great!" said Mrs. Casssidy. "And one more thing."

"Yes?"

"Stop down here in the Nursing Office in about fifteen minutes. There's something I have to discuss with you."

Courtney couldn't imagine what this could be about, but she agreed and hung up the phone.

She made a quick set of rounds to make sure everyone was all right and that they all had enough fluid in their I.V. bags to last until she got back. Then she informed Wanda the Ward Clerk where she was going.

"Hold on a minute," Wanda called to her as she headed for the door. "I got an order on this chart that I don't understand."

"Let me see," Courtney said with a confidence she didn't really feel. "It looks like it says A.M.F."

"That's what I thought. What's A.M.F., some kind of new lab test?" Courtney couldn't believe that Wanda was actually asking her opinion of something and treating her as an equal instead of some dumb new nurse.

"I have to get to the Nursing Office. Mrs. Cassidy's waiting for me. Why don't you call the intern and ask him what it means. Maybe they wrote it wrong."

"Uh uh, honey, you the nurse. I don't take no orders from doctors."

"But it's just a simple question. . . ."

"I ain't no nurse and I ain't takin no telephone orders. It's not in my job description."

Courtney gave up fighting a battle she knew she could never win and called the intern.

"Dr. Stern, I'm sorry to bother you. This is Courtney Quinn on 6-South. I have an order here on Mrs. Jennings, the fractured hip. I can't make out what it says. It looks like A.M.F."

"Oh, yeah," said Dr. Stern in a sleepy voice. "That's a discharge order."

"A.M.F.? I never heard of it. How do you get 'discharge' out of A.M.F.? Is it Latin or something?"

There was a hesitation on the other end of the line.

"Sort of. It stands for 'Adios, Mother Fucker.'" Click.

38

Courtney hung up the phone and peered into Wanda's expectant face.

"Well?" Wanda demanded.

"It means discharge." Courtney said flatly.

"I thought so," Wanda said, with a satisfied grin.

CHAPTER FOUR

"THE GREAT ESCAPE"

When Courtney reached the Nursing Office, what she saw confused and concerned her. Both the evening and night Nursing Supervisors were sitting behind a desk. Directly across from them, smoking a cigarette John Wayne style, was a Security Guard and across from him sat a man who looked like an administrator of some sort. They all wore concerned looks. The administrator-looking person beckoned Courtney to be seated.

Mrs. Cassidy made some perfunctory introductions and then gave the floor to Bob, the person Courtney had correctly guessed to be some type of administrator.

"I understand you've agreed to work the night shift up on 6-South tonight, Miss Quinn."

Courtney nodded.

"Good." He paused. "We seem to have a little problem tonight and we're going to need your cooperation." He then went on to explain the "little problem" as Courtney sat there wide-eyed, trying to take it all in.

He explained that there was a patient up on the sixteenth floor named Mr. Cook. Mr. Cook was a twenty-two-year-old member of a street gang who had been shot in the back earlier tonight as he was leaving the scene of a particularly violent fight between two rival gangs. The bullet had hit him at the T-12 level, leaving him paralyzed from the waist down. Ever since he had come back from surgery earlier this evening, he had been receiving threatening phone calls from the rival gang claiming that they knew where he was and that they were going to "finish him off."

Mr. Cook, of course, was in a state of panic. But no one was quite sure the threats were real, since Mr. Cook was the only one to hear them. . . and he had a psychiatric history of Paranoid Schizophrenia. Nonetheless, the hospital didn't want to take any chances, and gave the patient an alias, "Joseph Webster," and decided to transfer him to another floor. . . just in case. The floor they were going to send him to was 6-South.

Since all the beds on 6-South were full, it was decided that an extra bed would be brought up and put in the Nurses' Conference Room for "Mr. Webster." Courtney was instructed not to discuss this with anyone, including the three Nurses' Aids she would be working with. They were to be told simply that the hospital was overcrowded and that 6-South would have to take an extra patient in their Conference Room.

The administrator re-introduced Hank, the Security Guard, as Courtney sat there, wide-eyed and speechless. Hank stood up, lit another cigarette, leaned cockily against the door and blew the smoke up to the ceiling, the way they do in television squad rooms. He cleared his throat, looked directly at Courtney and began to speak in a gruff and gravelly voice.

"Now, Miss Quinn, this is a potentially dangerous situation, but I don't want you to be frightened. Nor do I want you to do anything foolish." As if she would.

He began to pace the room at this point, the way all the tough T.V. cops do. He had everyone's undivided attention and he was loving it. He continued.

"Rest assured that I'll have some of my men posted very close to 6-South all night long."

Courtney had seen many of the hospital Security Guards and she did not feel reassured. There was only one she had seen who looked like he weighed more than 150 pounds... and he only had one arm. Hank went on, loving the sound of his own voice.

"Of course, we won't be right on 6-South because we don't want to be obvious and give away the patient's location. Therefore, if you hear any strange noises or suspect anything at all, **don't**, under any circumstances, **DO NOT** investigate. At that point I want you to lock yourself in the Medication Room and call me from the phone in there. It's extension 4058. Understand?"

"Yes." Courtney answered like a good little girl in Catholic school, who would never question authority. Even if her very life were in danger.

Courtney made her way back to 6-South to prepare for Mr. Cook's - whoops - Mr. Webster's arrival. She saw the familiar form of Lulu, the Housekeeping lady from the other night, in the Conference Room making up a new bed.

"Hi," she said to the hardworking woman.

"Well, look who's here," she smiled in recognition. "Dr. Dave's friend. Did you enjoy those sandwiches the other night?"

"I sure did. Thank you very much."

"I'd do anything for Dr. Dave. I was wondering where you worked. I never seen you before. You must be new."

"Yeah, I guess I'm pretty new. And this place is so huge I'm surprised you even notice new people around here."

"Honey, when you been here as long as I have, you notice everything. Dr. Dave, boy, he kills me. I mighta known he'd notice a pretty new nurse like you before anyone else does."

Courtney didn't know just how to take that statement. She changed the subject. "Here, let me help you make up this bed."

"Ain't it time for you to go home, darlin'?"

"No, I'm doing a double shift tonight."

"Don't tell me those bastards talked you into staying tonight, what

42

with that crazy street gang patient coming. I heard the other gang's been threatening to finish him off tonight."

Courtney was astounded. Did **anything** escape this hospital grapevine? So much for Hospital Security.

About an hour later the patient arrived. Though partially paralyzed and quite heavily medicated, he was animated and panic-stricken. The orderly helped Courtney slide him onto the bed from the stretcher. The bottom half of his body was like that of a dead man. He chattered incessantly, never stopping for air, never waiting for an answer to his endless string of questions.

"They ain't gonna find me here, Nurse, are they? You gonna keep some Security Guards near me all night, aren't ya? You not gonna leave me alone back here, are ya?"

After "Mr. Webster" was settled in, still highly anxious and talkative, Courtney went outside to pour her twelve midnight medications. She added a 5 mg. tablet of Valium to Mr. Webster's medications. It had been ordered 'p.r.n.' (as needed) and, God knows, he needed it.

As soon as he heard Courtney's footsteps approaching his room, his wild eyes were open and he began his one-sided tirade. His body was like a big, human machine gun, his mouth spitting out a constant stream of words like bullets. And his brain seemed to have a never ending supply of paranoid schizophrenic ammunition.

Courtney put the tray of medications down on his bedside table with deliberate calmness. She poured him a glass of water and gave him the Valium first. He was quiet only for the four seconds it took to swallow the pill. Then his constant chatter resumed.

"Nurse, I just heard a noise out in the hall. You gotta check it out, please! I can't run, man. You gotta help me. You gotta make sure no one's around out there! Please, Nurse, please go make sure no one's out there!"

His panic was contagious. Courtney tried not to let it affect her, but it wasn't easy. "Mr. Webster," Courtney said in her most reassuring voice, "I just came from out there and believe me, there is no one out there."

"No, you don't understand. They gonna kill me! Shhh. . . listen. . . you hear that? I know they're out there. Please, Nurse, please, don't let them find me." He was begging her.

"Mr. Webster, you're getting yourself all worked up over nothing. You are perfectly safe here." But Courtney's words weren't even reassuring herself anymore. She strained her ears to hear the sound of footsteps Mr. Webster swore were out in the hallway, but all she could hear was the pounding of her heart.

"Nurse, please!" he insisted. His eyes were bulging now and darting back and forth with terror. "You don't know what they're like! They want me dead and they won't stop looking 'till they find me! You gotta help me, please!" Beads of perspiration glistened on his face under the dim light of Courtney's flashlight. "Please, Nurse, call somebody before they come back here and finish me off."

At that precise moment, they both heard the creak of the big heavy door that separated 6-South from the rest of the hospital. Courtney froze. Both she and Mr. Webster stared mutely at each other, each of them turning visibly paler.

Courtney's heart sank as she realized there was no telephone in this room. The Maintenance man had removed it yesterday because it wasn't working. Oh, God. The only thing she could think to do was to walk into the hallway nonchalantly and get to the phone at the desk as unobtrusively as possible. When she found her voice, it was quivering, so she tried to control it by lowering it a few octaves.

"Mr. Webster," she said in as soothing a voice as possible. "I'm going out to the desk to call Security. I'm sure there's no one out there, but I'll call them just to make you feel better." She was lying through her teeth, but apparently Mr. Webster was too caught up in his own panic to catch on. Courtney was certain someone had just entered that hallway.

44

"O.K., Nurse," he whispered. "But please don't leave me alone too long."

Courtney patted his hand reassuringly, picked up her tray laden with medications for the rest of the floor, and soundlessly left. Her heart was pounding in her ears and her fingers were icy, but she knew it would be more dangerous to hide in the back with Mr. Webster. Their only chance was for Courtney to get to a phone. . . quickly. She heard the creak of that door opening - there was no doubt in her mind about that - and there was no reason for any of the Nurses' Aides to leave the unit. They were supposed to be answering patient call lights while Courtney passed out the medications. Someone had undoubtedly entered the ward.

Courtney put on the most nonchalant facial expression she could muster and entered the dimly lit corridor. It was eerily quiet and empty, but nothing seemed amiss. She quickened her step as she walked past linen closets and the darkened kitchen - places where an intruder could easily hide. The Nurses' Station was in view now. She had only a few more steps to go before she could reach for the phone on the desk.

That's when an icy hand landed on her shoulder and she heard herself let out a terrified scream as her medication tray hurled through the air, scattering pills and syringes in all directions.

"Miss Quinn! Get hold of yourself!" the Night Supervisor's voice commanded. Courtney turned to see the stern face studying her. She was speechless with relief and suddenly she simply had to cry. The Night Supervisor's expression softened and she put her arm around Courtney's quivering shoulders. "There, there," she soothed, "I'm sorry I startled you. I should have known you'd be nervous."

"I'm not usually nervous," Courtney blubbered, "but Mr. Webster and I heard that old wooden door creak and Mr. Webster insisted it was those men who are after him and I couldn't imagine who'd be coming through that door at this hour."

"I understand, dear," her voice was kind. "It's all right now. I've been in touch with Security and there's been no sign of any unauthorized people around. I was just coming to see how you were doing."

Courtney glanced down at the multi-colored pills and contaminated syringes that were littering the hallway and she laughed through her tears. "I don't think I'm doing very well," she observed as she pictured herself cleaning up this mess and re-pouring all those medications.

The Supervisor smiled and advised Courtney to try to relax. Courtney didn't know how long she was supposed to do that with the possibility of a gang war on the ward and the fact that she was at least an hour behind schedule in her work. The Supervisor said she would stop back later, but that she would announce herself first.

Courtney saw the light go on over Tommy Matthews' door. The Nurses' Aide answered it over the intercom.

"Can I help you?"

"I want to talk to Courtney. Is she still here?"

"Yes, but she's very busy. Can I help you?"

"I want to talk to Courtney," came the annoyed reply.

Then Courtney remembered how she had told Tommy she would try to stop back and hear him play another song on his guitar. She thought about how his minutes must seem like hours. And how her hours flew by like minutes.

"It's O.K.," Courtney said to the Nurses' Aid. "Tell him I'll be there in a couple of minutes."

Courtney finished passing out medications to everyone on the floor except for Tommy and his new roommate, Michael. She saved theirs for last so that, hopefully, she could spend a little of her precious time with them. Unfortunately, it was two o'clock in the morning. Fortunately, they were both still awake.

"I thought you left," came a small voice in the dark as Courtney entered the room.

"No, I'm gonna be here all night. I'm sorry I didn't get back here earlier," she whispered, "but I've been awfully busy."

"You don't have to whisper, I'm awake too," said Michael from the other side of the room.

"Great. Does that mean Tommy can play one more song for me on his guitar?" she asked.

"I thought you forgot." There was hurt in Tommy's voice.

"Forget you?" Courtney said with exaggerated enthusiasm. "Are you kidding? I've been looking forward to this all night. I just got busy, that's all."

"What'd I tell you?" chirped Michael.

Tommy played the guitar softly in the dark and Courtney sat on the side of his bed spellbound. How could anyone think this child was a problem? He was a delightful little boy who was bravely suffering through a disease that even people who criticized him couldn't have coped with. Tommy was special. Courtney could see that. And so, she thought, could his roommate. Michael encouraged Tommy to sing and told him what a good voice he had. Courtney was glad she met the two of them. Life had been terribly unfair to these two boys. She wondered what kind of Catholic explanation Sister Mary Michael or any nun or priest would have given to this situation. No doubt it would have had something to do with how noble it is to suffer here on earth so that you will have a wonderful afterlife. Somehow these explanations were growing weak in light of all the daily tragedies she was witnessing these days.

Once again, Courtney had to leave because she had a lot of work to do. But Tommy looked happy now and Michael looked tired. She bid them goodnight and went out to the desk to start her paperwork.

The night was flying by. At five o'clock Courtney sat down for the first time and slid her shoes off her aching feet and propped a pillow behind the small of her aching back. Her body was obviously not happy about having been on its feet for almost sixteen hours now. Suddenly she wondered how the older nurses did it. She'd watched them work double shifts, especially around Christmas time, and never thought much about it. But now she wondered how it would feel to be doing this when she was fifty.

The telephone rang, interrupting her thoughts, and she grabbed it on the first ring so as not to awaken any patients. It was the Nursing Supervisor. Her voice was soft and calm. "Miss Quinn? How are you, dear?"

Courtney couldn't help but chuckle as she realized this woman was probably afraid to make rounds again on 6-South. She probably figured it was safer to call. It was a device known to Nursing Supervisors, interns and residents as "telephone rounds."

"I'm fine," Courtney answered.

"Good." Then the voice grew crisper. "I'm afraid I have some disturbing news," she continued. "I'm afraid Security has reason to believe that Mr. Webster isn't completely crazy. They just received a phone call in Administration threatening his life again."

Courtney noticed goose flesh appear on her arms.

The Supervisor continued. "We're going to transfer him to a hospital in Boston. All the arrangements have been made and Security wants to get him out of here before daybreak."

Courtney was instructed to pack up the patient's personal belongings as quickly as possible without saying a word to anyone. She was also to gather his chart, medications and a few extra bags of I.V. fluid and get him on a stretcher. Someone, probably the Night Supervisor, would be up shortly to help Courtney get him down to the Emergency Room where an ambulance would be waiting to take him to Boston.

Courtney's hands were shaking as she packed her patient's

48

medications, making sure to send plenty of Valium with him. She finished up her Nurse's Notes on him as the Nurses' Aides eyed her suspiciously, but asked no questions. As promised, the Nursing Supervisor arrived on the ward to help pull Mr. Webster's big body, with the lifeless legs, onto the stretcher. Mr. Webster obviously knew what was going on but was too frightened to ask questions. They spoke softly and reassuringly to him, but they couldn't hide their concern as the first traces of dawn stretched across the sky. The two nurses pushed the stretcher quickly and wordlessly through the labyrinth of corridors on the ground floor that led to the Emergency Room. There was absolutely no conversation, not even from Mr. Webster, as the nurses quickened their pace, looking back and forth behind them every few seconds.

When they reached the E.R., Hank the Security Guard was standing in the doorway, holding a walkie-talkie. "O.K., they're here now," he said softly into it, then accompanied them to the ambulance entrance. He punched the button on the wall and the automatic doors slid open, exposing them to the first pink glow of morning and the bone-chilling, January wind. An ambulance was sitting there with the doors open, like a mother with open arms, waiting to embrace and protect her child. Two paramedics suddenly appeared and lifted the stretcher into the back of the ambulance. Courtney reached up and slowed the I.V. to a K.V.O (Keep Vein Open) rate for the long ride. Suddenly the doors slammed closed and Courtney stood there for a moment watching the ambulance slip silently into its escape to Boston.

Courtney glanced at her watch. It was almost six-thirty. The day shift would be dragging in any minute now, eyes still swollen with sleep, carrying Styrofoam cups of steaming coffee. Courtney was unbearably tired.

"I know you'll never get out of here on time," the Supervisor said. "Make sure you give me a call when you're leaving so I can make sure to put you down for overtime. By the way, are you working again this afternoon?"

"Yes," Courtney answered numbly, "I have to be back at three."

"Well, try to get some sleep," she said, then walked off in the

49

direction of the Nursing Office.

As Courtney returned to 6-South, the phone was ringing. Automatically, she picked it up. She hadn't learned yet to avoid the phone when her shift was ending.

"6-South, Miss Quinn speaking."

"Miss Quinn?" came David Strauss' surprised voice. "What are you doing there at this hour?"

"I worked a double last night," she said wearily.

"Well, no wonder I couldn't get hold of you. I called you last night and, when you didn't answer, I figured you must be out carousing."

"I was carousing, all right," she laughed, "up and down these halls all night."

"Well, what do you say we get together one of these evenings? Mark Duffy's having a party at his house Friday night. Would you like to go?"

Courtney was thrilled. What a great ending to this terrible night. "I don't know who Mark Duffy is but, sure, I'd love to go."

"Atta girl," Dave laughed. "We'll plan the details later. I'll call you. Meanwhile, do me a favor and write an N.P.O. order on Doris White in 672. We might be taking her to the O.R. later."

Courtney left work that morning walking on air. A real date with the charming Dave Strauss. Wait until she told Karen. And, best of all, finally . . . at long last . . . she was beginning to feel like a real nurse.

CHAPTER FIVE

"HOLD THE MAYO"

It seemed like Courtney had only just put her head down when the alarm went off. It was one o'clock in the afternoon. That gave her just enough time to shower, grab a bite to eat, iron a uniform and get to work. One good thing about working 3 to 11 was that she never had to battle Philadelphia's Center City rush hour traffic.

She automatically flicked on the television. There wasn't much on at this hour of the day except the soap operas. She had to chuckle as she realized how many of those shows revolved around a hospital setting. She listened only half-heartedly as she prepared her "breakfast" and plugged in the iron. But then she began to get a little irritated with this highly inaccurate and romanticized view of Nursing. She looked closely at the actresses who portrayed nurses and noticed that each one was more buxom than the next. Name pins were worn uniformly over the left nipple, practically poking the T.V. viewer (not to mention the "doctors") in the eye. Dark stockings and high heels completed their outfits and, in between gossip sessions, they made a big deal about bringing one pill down the hall to one patient. She hoped the public didn't really believe this version of Nursing.

She went about preparing herself to go to work, but she couldn't get the thought of that soap opera out of her mind. Their portrayal of nurses was degrading and damaging. Someone should say something. **She** would say something. She took out a piece of writing paper and scribbled off a short but resentful note to the producers of the show and another one to the sponsors, vowing that she would never buy their products until they portrayed nurses, and women in general, with the respect they deserve. The baby tiger in her heart was learning to roar.

. . . . .

51

Courtney didn't have time to wait for the elevator when she arrived at work. She was running a little late. Instead she took the back stairs which emptied her out in front of the Radiology Department. She saw a familiar looking form sitting in a wheelchair wearing a Pittsburgh Pirates baseball cap. She walked quietly up behind him, then tugged the cap down over his face. Tommy grabbed the hat, ready for a fight, then recognized Courtney and smiled.

"You're back again tonight?" he said, not trying to hide his delight.

"Yup. And you better be nice to me 'cause I'm tired and cranky."

"I won't cause you any trouble," he said earnestly.

Courtney's heart melted at his sincerity. "I'm only teasing. You can cause as much trouble as you want. I'll just ignore you." They both laughed, understanding that each of them had found a new friend.

"What are you doing here anyway?" Courtney asked, thinking that she didn't remember seeing any x-rays ordered for him last night.

"Oh, Dr. Shapiro said he heard some rales in both my lungs. He thinks I might have some atelectasis in my right lower lobe," Tommy answered matter-of-factly, with a straight face.

"Listen to all these five dollar words coming from a guy whose idea of literature is an Incredible Hulk comic book."

Courtney pulled the brim of his baseball cap down over his eyes again and he laughed this time. It wasn't fair that a fifteen-year-old boy, so full of life and mischief should have words like "atelectasis" and "rales" in his vocabulary. His childlike sincerity washed over her heart with a sweetness that made even these sterile hallways seem warm.

"Are you married?" he asked from out of the blue.

"Why? Are you proposing?"

He blushed. "No, I just bet you're not married, that's all."

52

"How do you know?" Courtney queried, a bit intrigued.

"`Cause you work the 3 to 11 shift."

"What does that prove?"

"Everybody knows that only the single ones and the divorced ones work that shift," he answered smugly. "You're not divorced are you?"

"No, I'm not married and no, I'm not divorced. I'm too young for any of that stuff," she said only half jokingly.

"How old are you anyway?" He asked without even the slightest hesitation. If Tommy wanted to know something, he simply asked. No holds barred.

"I'm twenty-two."

"Wow, You're plenty old enough to be married."

"Are you always this blunt?"

"What does 'blunt' mean?"

"Look it up. It comes right after 'atalectasis' in the dictionary." Courtney looked at her watch as she laughed. "Listen, I gotta run. I'm gonna be late. I'll see you back at the fort."

. . . . .

Courtney was getting used to Maggie Ruggles' loud voice arguing with someone every time she entered the ward. If she didn't hear it one day, she'd probably think she was on the wrong floor. "Get your hands out of there!" Maggie scolded a rather nice looking resident who was reaching for a piece of chocolate candy.

"Ah, c'mon, Maggie, just one piece. Please?"

"What did you do to earn it?" she demanded. "You guys kill me. We do all the work, the patient gives us a box of candy and you guys just come along and assume it belongs to you, too."

"Well, I pinned her hip," he said with confidence.

"Well, I cleaned her shit. Top that, wise guy."

The resident suddenly looked up and seemed to be amazed at something behind Maggie. Maggie turned around and the resident grabbed a handful of chocolate candy and walked away laughing. "Thanks, Mag Pie. You're too generous."

"Mark Duffy, you're gonna pay," she called after him.

So that was Mark Duffy. He was cute. And funny. Courtney guessed he must be an Orthopedic resident since he claimed to have "pinned" a hip. She was really beginning to look forward to Friday. Thank God she didn't have to work. And she didn't have to go in the next day 'til three o'clock, so she could stay out as late as she wanted and wouldn't have to worry about getting up in the morning. Maybe Tommy knew what he was talking about.

"One of these days," Maggie was grumbling, "I'm going to come up with an invention that will make me a millionaire and get me out of this rat race forever."

"Well, I sure like your last invention," piped up Wanda the Ward Clerk as she arrived, ten minutes late, for work.

"Which one was that?" Maggie asked. "I forget."

"You know, 'The Crap Trap.' The big thick tube that goes up the butt and has suction on it and pulls the stool out into a disposable plastic bag that's hooked to the bedside."

"Oh, yeah," said Maggie, "that was a good one."

54

Courtney couldn't believe her ears. But the worst part was that she didn't know whether or not to take them seriously.

"But that wasn't as good as the book I was going to write for quadriplegics," Maggie suddenly remembered.

"How did that go?" asked Wanda "I forget what that was about."

"I was going to call it Suicide Maneuvers for Quadriplegics, or A Hundred and One Ways to Kill Yourself Even Though You're Paralyzed. Trouble is, I could only think of twenty-eight ways to do it. I bet it would have been a big success though."

Courtney felt sick. She didn't care what Dave said. This Maggie Ruggles was a sick cookie. Why didn't she just get out of Nursing if she hated it so much?

Report began and Courtney stifled yawns all the way through it. That double shift last night had apparently taken its toll. Maggie came in the Conference Room as soon as report was finished and said to the 3 to 11 staff, "Oh, just one more thing. What do you know about M.A.O. Inhibitor diets?"

"It's a special diet for people who are taking certain anti-depressant drugs." Courtney remembered this from school and was only too happy to show Maggie that she did know something.

"Very good," said Maggie, trying to suppress the surprise in her voice. "And what happens if they're given any of the wrong foods like cheese, or chocolate or wine or yogurt?"

Courtney was quick to answer. "They go into a hypertensive crisis."

"Very good, Quinn," said Maggie with a note of respect in her voice. "Well, I'm glad you're such an expert on this subject because Mr. Colosi in 649 is on an M.A.O. Inhibitor diet and the kitchen's been sending him the wrong stuff on his meal trays all day. He hasn't eaten a thing. I called the kitchen and yelled at them, but I don't know what good it'll do. I also called Linda Reynolds, the head Dietician, and she assures me that Mr. Colosi will get his proper tray for dinner. Just make sure you check any tray before it goes in his room. I still don't trust those illiterates who work in the kitchen."

The 3 to 11 shift rose and filed out the door to begin their routine. Maggie grabbed Courtney's arm just as she was about to leave and pulled her back.

"What did you do to Tommy Matthews last night? He's like a different person. And all he talked about is 'Courtney Quinn.'"

"I treated him like a human being." Courtney was no longer afraid of Maggie.

"And I suppose it was your idea to give him a roommate, that McClendon guy?"

"Yes. It was my idea." Courtney was prepared for an argument.

Maggie was quiet for a moment as she studied Courtney's face. "Good work," she said, and walked out the door.

The evening wore on in what was beginning to become a routine for Courtney. There were admissions, and patients coming back from the O.R. and irate visitors complaining about the "service" around here. Dinner trays arrived and the first thing Courtney did was make a bee line for Mr. Colosi's room so that she could check his tray before he ate any of the wrong food.

Once again, Mr. Colosi had received foods that could kill him. His mouth was watering as Courtney swiped the plate of cheese ravioli and yogurt from under his nose. "I'm sorry, Mr. Colosi," she apologized, "but I can't let you have this food. The kitchen made another mistake. I'll get you a new tray in just a few minutes.

"Goddammit!" Mr. Colosi bellowed. "Doesn't anyone in this place know what they're doing? I come here to get better and you people end up starving me to death!"

Courtney couldn't argue with him. He was right. She went out to the desk and called Dietary. "This is the third time today that you people have given this patient a meal that could have killed him." She noticed that she sounded frighteningly like Maggie Ruggles.

"Yeah, yeah. We hear that all the time," replied the Dietary Aide.

"This is very serious," Courtney chided. "Let me speak to a supervisor." It felt good to yell at somebody else when you knew you were a hundred percent right. Oh God. What was happening to her?

"This is Mrs. Fisher, can I help you?" came a calm, yet efficient voice.

Courtney went on to tell the story again and the importance of avoiding certain foods for this patient. "Do you know what an M.A.O. Inhibitor diet is?" she demanded.

"Yes, I do," came the placid reply. "We'll send another tray up right away."

Twenty minutes later , a Dietary Aide arrived at the desk carrying a dinner tray for Mr. Colosi. He handed Courtney the tray and left quickly. Apparently word had spread that 6-South was hostile territory Courtney opened the tray to check it before putting it in front of poor Mr. Colosi again. What she saw made her blood boil. Once again, it had all the foods that were restricted from the patient's diet. An identification tag fell from the tray. . .Courtney picked it up off the floor and was dumbfounded by what it said:

Gerald Colosi
Room 649
HOLD THE MAYO

CHAPTER SIX

"THE SOCIAL SIDE"

You could hear the music from Mark Duffy's party within a one block radius of the house. No need to ring the doorbell, no one would have heard it anyway. Dave opened the door as if he lived there and a blast of rock 'n' roll music enveloped them on the front porch. Dave took Courtney's hand and led her through the crowd. There were wall-to-wall people, all laughing and drinking and shouting to be heard. There was a keg of beer in the kitchen and, oddly enough, a bunch of people standing around eating oranges. There were beer-filled I.V. bags hanging from portable I.V. poles with people, mostly residents, sucking the end of the tubing and thoroughly enjoying themselves. This was a lot different from the way they looked at the hospital. Once again, Dave was introducing her to a world that was completely foreign to her.

"At least it's a pretty health conscious crowd," Courtney noted.

"What makes you say that?" Dave sounded almost dismayed.

"All those people in the kitchen eating oranges," she said.

Dave laughed. "Oh, that." He paused for a moment, then asked, "Would you like one?"

"O.K.," she said agreeably, though she thought it odd for people to be eating fresh fruits at a party. But then, these were mostly health care professionals, so who was to say. She bit into the orange. It tasted good. She finished it and started on another one as Dave drank a beer from the keg and made his way over to Mark Duffy. Mark was wearing O.R. greens and drinking what looked to be a coke. So many odd scenarios in this place. Dave finally pulled Mark over and introduced him to Courtney. He shook her hand and asked if he didn't see her on 6-South the other day when he was stealing chocolate candy from under Maggie Ruggles' nose.

"Yes, I was there," Courtney laughed.

"I thought that was you," Mark said with a lopsided grin.

"Mark's an Orthopedic resident," Dave interjected. "It takes a real man to be an Ortho resident," he teased as he playfully punched Mark's shoulder.

"Eat your heart out, pal," Mark laughed.

"Yeah, you have to be strong as an ox . . . and twice as smart," Dave laughed at his friend.

"Yeah, well everybody knows what a bunch of perverts you OB/GYN guys are. Courtney, you better watch out for this guy."

Courtney was thoroughly enjoying this playful banter between two good friends. She felt wonderful.

"Now who's eating his heart out, pal?" continued Dave. "Besides, you know what else they say about you Ortho guys?"

"No. What else do 'they' say? Careful, though, you might hurt my delicate doctor's ego."

Dave took a slug of his beer. "To be an Orthopod, you have to be smarter than a rock, but not quite as smart as a tree."

Mark laughed good-naturedly, then countered with "Yeah, well, I'll laugh all the way to the bank over that one." Then he turned to Courtney and said, "Hey, Courtney, how do you like those oranges? Pretty good, huh?"

"Yeah, they're great," Courtney gushed. "I've never tasted anything quite like them."

"I'm glad all my hard work paid off," Mark laughed, as Dave shot him a high sign.

Too late.

"Hard work? How can oranges be any work to prepare?" Courtney asked all wide-eyed and innocent. God, she felt wonderful.

"Well, first you gotta rip off the syringes from the hospital, and then you could spend a good part of the afternoon injecting them." Mark answered in all sincerity.

"Injecting them?" Courtney was astounded. And scared.

"Yeah, you know, with vodka."

"Vodka?" No wonder she felt wonderful. And here she thought they were all a bunch of health freaks. But she really did feel awfully good. It took a moment, but then she broke into a smile. What the hell. She felt great. "What a great idea," she said, to Dave's relief.

The music was loud and inviting and suddenly Dave wanted to dance. Normally, Courtney would have been a bit inhibited, but with a couple of those oranges under her belt, she was ready for anything. It must have been all that Vitamin C.

Dave was a wonderful dancer and Courtney thoroughly enjoyed being held by him. He guided her expertly and effortlessly to the rhythm and she wished she could just freeze this moment in time. She looked up at him and he smiled at her. "Somehow I never expected a doctor to have such rhythm," she remarked.

Dave threw his head back and laughed as he spun her around. "Musicians usually have a good sense of rhythm," he laughed.

"Are you a musician too? What do you play?"

"Mostly the keyboard, but I like the saxophone, too."

"I had no idea!" She was incredulous.

"There's a lot you don't know about me, Miss Quinn. By the way, you're a pretty good dancer yourself."

"I didn't go to college for nothing, ya know," she quipped.

The song ended and a nervous-looking little resident approached them. Courtney had seen him before in the hospital but she didn't know who he was. He always appeared anxious and hyper, and tonight apparently was no exception.

"Hey, Dave," he said as he hyperventilated, "there's a tank upstairs if you want some. It's really a good time."

Courtney had no idea what this little man was talking about, but it struck her as funny that he would be able to recognize a good time when he saw one. He was gone before Dave could introduce them.

"Who was that?" Courtney asked.

"Oh, that's Hyper Al," he laughed.

"Hyper Al? I thought that was some kind of a thick solution you give to patients who need more calories than they can take in by mouth. Yeah. Hyperalimentation, right? Hyperal for short."

"Yeah, but don't go and get medical on me. We're at a party. Al's a Medical resident. He never really was hyper until, one night during his internship year, they called a code on some old guy. In fact, I think it was on your floor. It was three o'clock in the morning and Al was asleep in the On-Call Room. He must have misunderstood the room number they announced and he went running to the wrong room. He sees this old G.O.R.K. laying in the bed, with his mouth gaping open and his tongue hanging out. He claims he felt for a carotid pulse and didn't feel anything, so he jumps on the bed and starts C.P.R. figuring the rest of the code team will be along in a minute. It turns out, the team was across the hall coding the right patient and here's old Al pumping on this guy's chest, who's just sleeping. Well I guess it's kind of hard to sleep when some nut suddenly jumps on your bed, gives you two breaths and starts beating on your chest. The guy died and Al's been hyperventilating ever since. That's why we call him 'Hyper Al.'"

Courtney was spellbound by this story. By how easily a tragic mistake can be made.

"What did the patient die of?" She asked, horrified.

"Heart attack. Must have scared him to death. Al broke a few ribs too during the chest compressions and punctured a lung."

"What happened? Didn't anyone find out and sue him?"

"Nah, Al was lucky. The guy didn't have any family and the code team came over when they finished resuscitating the real patient and put on a show. Just for the record."

Courtney didn't know if she'd ever stop being shocked by this profession. Even at a party with Vodka-spiked oranges, she was still learning profound lessons about the career she had chosen.

"C'mon. Let's go upstairs and have part of that tank."

"What are you talking about? What tank?"

"Nitrous Oxide. You know, Laughing Gas. It's fun."

"Dave, I hate to sound like a prude, but I've never done anything like that before and quite frankly, it scares me."

"There's nothing to be afraid of. Trust me. I wouldn't let anything hurt you. It's the same thing you get when you go to the dentist to relax you. And the beauty of it is that as soon as you start breathing room air, you come right down. No hangover, no regrets. Just one good time. I bet that's where Mark is right now. He's on call tonight, so he can't get drunk or high. Nitrous is perfect. It makes you feel good, and then you come right back to normal within five or ten minutes. C'mon. It'll be fun."

Courtney was in no mood to protest. She felt too good from those two oranges she'd eaten. "Life with you is an education . . . and a constant adventure," she added, then followed him up the stairs.

There was a group of people sitting in a circle on the floor in Mark's bedroom. As predicted, Mark was among them. There was a big green cylinder tank in the middle of the circle with some oxygen tubing attached to it. People were sucking in on the tubing for a moment, then passing it on to the person beside them. It seemed to be a happy group and there was a lot of laughing going on.

Dave and Courtney joined the group. Courtney watched Dave suck on the tube, then followed suit when her turn came. She had to admit it felt good. Suddenly anything that anyone said seemed hysterically funny. Mark's beeper went off, and everyone laughed, but no one knew why. Mark got up to answer his page and little by little the group broke up . Even Hyper Al seemed to have had enough to slow his breathing to an almost normal rate. Upon realizing he was the only one in the room besides Courtney and Dave, he began hyperventilating and excused himself.

At that point Mark Duffy walked into the room to get his coat.

"Where ya goin', buddy?" asked Dave.

"Oh, I gotta go over to the hospital for a minute. Keep an eye on things here for me, will ya? I shouldn't be long."

"You can take 'call' from home?" Courtney asked, incredulous. "What if there's an emergency?"

Mark laughed.

"One of the first rules an Orthopedic nurse learns is never to call the Ortho resident 'stat.' There is no such thing as an Orthopedic emergency."

"What about a patient with a fractured hip who suddenly develops chest pain?" Courtney wanted to know.

"Transfer to Medicine. Let the F.L.E.A.s. worry about it."

63

Mark and Dave laughed ruefully at that answer.

"Besides," teased Dave, "everybody knows the Orthopods don't know anything about the heart."

"That's right," agreed Mark good-naturedly, "all we know about the heart is that it pumps Ancef to the bones."

Mark walked out the door laughing, then stuck his head back in and said, "You better watch this guy, Courtney. He's one of those perverted OB/GYN guys. No telling what he'll do now that he's got you alone."

"Don't give me any ideas," said Dave.

Courtney was pensive for a moment.

"You know, I really should take that E.K.G. course that's coming up. We seem to have quite a few codes on our floor and I have no idea how to read those E.K.G. strips."

"Why should you have to? They have technicians and nurses who do nothing else, and at least one of them is always on the code team."

"But I really don't know enough about the heart. I'd honestly like to learn more."

"The only important thing to learn about the heart is not to get it broken."

"Do I detect a note of bitterness?" Courtney asked.

"Certainly not." Dave smiled. "Go ahead and take the E.K.G. course if it makes you feel better. I just don't see why you need it."

"Because I want to know what I'm doing. I want to be a well-rounded professional. I don't want to be like one of those soap opera nurses."

"Soap opera nurses? What are you talking about?"

Courtney told him the story of what she'd seen on T.V. the other day and how degraded she had felt. She told him how she had written them a letter and was boycotting the products that the sponsors sold.

"Oh, Courtney," he sighed. "Don't you ever get tired of trying to change the world?"

"No." She said flatly. "And, furthermore, you ain't seen nothin' yet."

He looked at her for a moment.

"You're such a little rebel."

"I can't help it, Dave. When I see a situation that needs to be changed, I can't rest until I know I've at least done my part to change it. If that's being a rebel then, O.K., I guess I'm a rebel."

Dave tilted her chin and brought his face close to hers.

"Yes, but you're **my** little rebel," he whispered, just before he kissed her.

CHAPTER SEVEN

"THE TOE LADY"

Tommy Matthews hated to see his roommate go home. Michael was doing well and the exacerbation of his Lupus, for which he had been admitted, now seemed to be under control. That's why Tommy didn't particularly like having roommates. They always got better. And Tommy didn't. But Michael was different. He had become a friend and he and Tommy had spent many a night talking about things that only a terminally ill young guy could understand. Tommy was going to miss Michael.

But at least he still had Courtney. Even though she was a girl and wasn't terminally ill, she seemed to understand better than anybody else how hard it was to be trapped in this place. Plus she didn't pull any punches, especially when it came to talking about dying. Tommy was no fool. He knew his days were numbered. The worst part about a terminal illness, besides the obvious, is that no one ever lets you talk about dying. Especially when you're young. . . like Tommy. He couldn't help but notice how uncomfortable that subject makes people. He learned long ago that if you want your visitors to leave, just talk about the fact that you're dying. After they finish telling you not to talk like that and that you're going to get better, they practically leave skid marks on their way out. It can make a person feel awful lonesome. It can make a person be a pain in the ass - just to get even.

Michael wasn't officially discharged till late in the afternoon because there were a few more blood tests the doctors wanted to check before they let him go. He didn't leave until four o'clock when Courtney came in to tell him that everything looked good and the doctor had just called to say he could go. She handed Michael some prescriptions the doctor had left for him and told him to call if he had any questions or problems. Then she squeezed his hand and wished him well. There was an orderly standing in the doorway with a wheelchair waiting for him.

66

"Do I **have** to ride in that thing, Courtney?" he asked, pointing to the wheelchair. "it makes me feel like . . . like. . . ."

"Like a patient?" she asked, hitting the nail on the head.

They all laughed and Courtney picked up Michael's belongings and put them on the seat of the wheelchair.

"Promise me you won't fall . . . or tell anyone that I said it was all right to walk."

Tommy and Michael were both thinking the same thing: That the only good thing about being in the hospital was having Courtney for your nurse.

After Michael had left, Courtney informed Tommy that he'd be getting a new roommate later in the evening. A fourteen-year-old boy named Gary.

"What's he in for?" asked Tommy.

"Assault and Battery," cracked Courtney.

"No, really. What's he got?"

"Well, that's a little better. This isn't a prison, you know. He's got a little fatty lump on his leg and the doctor wants to remove it - just to be on the safe side."

Ordinarily Courtney would never discuss one patient's business with another. But Tommy had some pretty harrowing experiences with roommates in the past who were dreadfully sick and who kept him up all night and she knew this would ease his mind.

"Can you stop back in later, do you think? You know, maybe play a game of cards or something?"

Tommy looked lonesome already.

"I'll really try. In the meantime, you call me if you need anything," Courtney said as she prepared to get back to the mountain of work awaiting her in the Nurses' Station. But Tommy was telling her what he needed, she thought. It's just that Admitting Offices and Operating Rooms and insurance companies didn't see loneliness as a top priority. There wasn't any profit in it. And without profits, there wouldn't be a hospital.

When she reached the Nurses' Station, it was filled with half a dozen Orthopedic residents preparing to make rounds on the three overflow patients. These were patients who had Orthopedic surgery, but for whom there was no room on the regular Orthopedic floor, so they were sent to 6-South, a general Medical/Surgical floor.

Mark Duffy was among the group of residents that followed like a group of baby ducklings behind the Chairman of their department as they began their rounds. Mark winked at Courtney as he followed humbly along. The Chairman was Dr. Webber, who had a reputation for torturing and humiliating his residents as part of their training. It was a lot like Catholic school, Courtney thought.

All four telephones in the Nurses' Station were ringing and Wanda motioned to her to pick up one of the blinking lines. It was the Nursing Supervisor telling her that they would be getting an emergency admission in an hour or two. A cop. He had been shot by one of the street gangs and undoubtedly would need twenty-four-hour-a-day protection. There would be two uniformed policemen outside his door and at least one plainclothesman on the ward at all times. The hospital was to give out no information regarding this situation. The officer's bodyguards would be on the ward shortly to await his arrival.

As Courtney hung up the phone, she noticed an anxious looking Mark Duffy signalling for her attention.

"Courtney, you got a bucket and some peroxide? I need it quick!" Mark said with something close to panic in his voice.

Courtney quickly got him what he needed and marched down the hall beside him.

"What's wrong, Mark? You look scared to death."

"I am."

"What happened? Do you want me to get the crash cart?"

"Yeah, for Dr. Webber. He's gonna need it when he finds out we forgot we had Mrs. Johnson on your floor and we never changed her dressing after surgery."

"She's the lady with the bunionectomy and the osteotomy on her second and third toes, right?" Courtney asked, trying to refresh her own memory.

"Yeah. But we never looked under her dressing and the surgery was two days ago. And it doesn't smell good in there."

"Has Dr. Webber been in there yet?"

"No, he's still with the patient next door. I just remembered Mrs. Johnson as I was standing there. Hopefully, the foul smell is just some old drainage we should have cleaned off and nothing more."

Courtney suddenly felt guilty that none of the nurses had noticed the foul smell or the fact that the dressing hadn't been changed. But then there had been one night when Courtney hadn't even seen Mrs. Johnson. The old story again of short staffing and only the squeaky wheels getting the oil. Apparently Mrs. Johnson didn't squeak loud enough.

They entered her room and one of the other Ortho residents was carefully and deliberately removing the bandage which, by this time, was glued to the wound with old, dried blood and drainage. The patient clenched her teeth and grimaced as she tried to cooperate with the doctors. The last of the bandage was pulled off, and what they saw horrified them. Mrs. Johnson's third toe was black. It was dead. No one said a word. The patient was still grimacing from the pain of having a two-day-old dressing removed, and so she hadn't noticed yet that her toe was dead.

"Hand me that peroxide, will you, Courtney?" Mark asked with the slightest hint of tremor in his voice.

She handed him the bottle and the other resident held a bucket beneath the patient's foot as Mark poured the entire contents of the bottle over the necrotic toe. To everyone's horror, including the patient's, the toe dangled precariously for a moment then dropped into the bucket. You could hear a pin drop.

"Doctor? Was that my toe that just fell in the bucket?" Mrs. Johnson asked in an unbelieving voice.

"Well, Mrs. Johnson, uh . . . Dr. Webber will be right in to talk to you about that. In fact, why don't I just go get him right now?"

"Good idea," chirped the other resident. "I'll help you."

And they both headed out the door leaving Courtney and Mrs. Johnson to look at each other in utter disbelief.

"You what?" roared Dr. Webber.

His voice carried from halfway down the hall. This was immediately followed by hushed voices conferring in the hallway and Courtney wondered how in the world they were ever going to explain this to the patient.

At last Dr. Webber entered the room followed by his entourage of frightened little ducklings. There was going to be hell to pay, but everyone appeared calm and composed in front of the patient.

"Dr. Webber," Mrs. Johnson began, "my toe just fell off in that bucket."

Dr. Webber. cleared his throat.

"That's right, Mrs. Johnson. Sometimes that happens."

"Oh, it does?" she asked pleasantly, nothing but utter trust in her eyes as she looked up at Dr. Webber.

"Oh yes. We see it all the time," said Dr. Webber with enough confidence to be convincing. "It's like when you go to the dentist. You know how sometimes when your teeth are crooked, the dentist has to pull one in order to make the rest of them straight?"

Mrs. Johnson was all ears. "Yes, uh-huh."

"Well, that's what happened with your toe. We had to 'pull' one, but the rest of them are all straight now."

"Oh, I see, Doctor," acknowledged the patient, no longer upset.

It was hard to believe that people could be so easily pacified. It was amazing to see the kind of respect that doctors got for screwing up. Not that Courtney wanted to see them in trouble, but she couldn't help wondering what would have happened if it had been the nurses who had screwed up.

By the time things settled down and Courtney was just catching up on the new orders that had been written, she noticed that her new admission, Tommy's latest roommate, had arrived.

His name was Gary Evans and he was beautiful in the way that only fourteen-year-old boys can be beautiful. He had an athletic build and his skin had a healthy, outdoorsy glow to it. His hair was thick and brown and cut close to his head, another sign of his athletic lifestyle. He was the picture of glowing good health, and poor little Tommy looked even more frail by comparison. Maybe putting them in the same room hadn't been such a good idea after all.

Courtney did the usual Admitting interview with Gary while his parents were downstairs in the Admitting Office filling out the endless parade of paperwork. Gary was friendly and cooperative and very well informed about his upcoming surgery tomorrow. He was aware that the lump on the calf of his leg was thought to be a benign, fatty tumor, that it could be excised under local anesthesia and he probably would be able to go home the same day.

"Have you ever been to the Operating Room before, Gary?" Courtney asked.

"No," he said, looking just a bit nervous.

"It's a breeze," Tommy smugly assured him like the veteran that he was.

Courtney laughed. She could see Tommy was going to show Gary the ropes. Gary couldn't have asked for a better teacher.

"Well, you certainly have an expert here for a roommate," Courtney laughed. "Just don't let him teach you to be a little brat like he is," she joked, pulling Tommy's ever-present baseball cap down.

She went on to explain that Gary would be numb and that he would be given medication to relax him.

"By this time tomorrow night you'll be home showing all your girl friends your scar," Courtney predicted.

As usual, the evening flew by in a blur of activity. The cop who'd been shot came down from the O.R. and two uniformed police officers sat outside his doorway. Courtney knew there was another plainclothes cop around, but she couldn't distinguish him from the visitors. Then she noticed a thirtyish looking man wearing khaki pants and a blue shirt. His hair was cut short and he walked with the ease of a man who was in top shape. She supposed that was him. She watched him bend over to pick a newspaper off the floor and caught a glimpse of the gun at his waist. It was quickly camouflaged when he straightened up again and his jacket slid over it.

Courtney had always liked cops. They were always delightful patients, never asking for much, never complaining. Usually there was so much camaraderie among them that their buddies took care of most

72

of their needs, especially their needs for pizza and entertainment. She liked how they seemed to respect the nurses and tried to stay out of their way. They were forever telling funny stories and joking with each other. It was always a pleasure to have them around.

Courtney was getting a cup of coffee for herself and decided to get three more cups for the officers. Their love of coffee was legendary. She was met with smiles and thanks from the policemen guarding the doorway. Then she approached the plainclothesman and offered him the steaming cup. He looked at her with surprise and asked, "Do you give all the visitors coffee?"

"Oh, no," she smiled, "I was just giving it to the cops."

He looked a little disappointed. "How did you know I was a cop?"

"By the bulge in your pants," Courtney said innocently.

"Excuse me?"

Then realizing what she had said, Courtney blushed and tried to explain. "No, no. I . . . I mean, the gun. I saw the gun bulging when you bent over before."

The plainclothesman laughed and extended his hand to Courtney.

"I'm Paul Edwards," he said, "and I'm glad to see we have such an observant nurse taking care of our buddy."

CHAPTER EIGHT

"THE HEART OF THE MATTER"

Courtney's decision to take the E.K.G. course and to learn more about the heart was a good one. The class was given from nine a.m. until noon, Monday through Friday, for two weeks. It included a detailed study of the anatomy and physiology of the heart which led to a means of making sense of the E.K.G. What used to look like a foreign language to her was now beginning to be comprehensible and sometimes even predictable. And though this meant she had to wake up at seven-thirty in the morning after working until eleven-thirty the night before, she was very glad she was doing it. There was always so much to learn. She would never be bored in this job. Exhausted maybe, but never bored.

Besides, it gave her a chance to meet Dave for lunch and, occasionally, if the OB/GYN service was quiet enough, they ate at a little romantic restaurant in Center City like normal people. She was able to relax and take her time since she didn't have to be on duty at the hospital until three. She and Dave sometimes walked along Chestnut Street, window shopping and daydreaming and just plain being together.

One day at noon, just as she had finished her class and was waiting for Dave at the Information Desk, she saw a familiar form walk past on his way to the elevators.

"Michael?" she asked.

Michael McClendon broke into a smile when he recognized her.

"Courtney, I didn't recognize you with regular clothes on."

A woman standing beside him gave them both a rather startled look.

"I wasn't sure it was you either," Courtney laughed. "What are you doing here?"

"Well, I thought I'd come up and say hello to Tommy. I was in town taking care of some business and figured he could use the company."

"That's so nice of you, Michael. I know Tommy will appreciate it. His family's terrific, but I think he gets a little lonesome."

They stood at the elevators chatting for a few moments. Courtney couldn't help but notice how well Michael was looking. It was gratifying to see someone actually feeling well and functioning as a result of the medical care he had received. She couldn't help thinking what a nice person he was to take the time to go up and visit Tommy.

She felt an arm go around her shoulder and looked up into Dave's smiling face. She introduced the two men then bid Michael good-bye as she and Dave made their way out into Center City's lunch crowd.

They went to a restaurant that was fast becoming "their" place. It was dimly lit with Tiffany lamps on the tables and a fireplace in the center of the room that threw a flattering, golden light on the surroundings. The food was plentiful and not very expensive. Courtney loved sitting there with Dave. She didn't even mind his beeper going off as long as it was something that could wait for them to finish their lunch.

"Courtney Quinn, where have you been all my life?" Dave asked as he finished his burger and leaned back in his chair.

"Right here in Center City," she smiled.

"Do you have any idea how much I love being with you?"

"No, tell me. I want to know," she said, flattered.

Dave perused the dessert menu.

"Well, let's see now. I'd say I like being with you as much as I'd like being with this Suicide Chocolate Brownie Cake."

"Oooooh. That sounds good. Let's split one."

Dave laughed. He ordered the Suicide Chocolate Brownie Cake then reached across the table for Courtney's hand.

"I had a great time at Mark Duffy's party with you."

"Me, too. Even though you tried to take advantage of me by feeding me those spiked oranges," she laughed.

"It didn't hurt you any," he defended himself. "In fact, I think it actually helped loosen you up a little."

"Are you calling me a prude?"

"Certainly not. I think you're great. In fact, I want to kiss you right here and now."

"So go ahead," she dared.

"Not in public. Not the **way** I want to kiss you. We'd get arrested."

The waitress plopped the dessert down between them just then. They stared at each other for a moment.

"The On Call Room should be empty this time of day, shouldn't it?" Courtney asked mischievously.

Dave looked down at the cake then back to Courtney's inviting face. He dropped his fork, threw a twenty-dollar bill on the table and yanked Courtney from her seat. They half-walked, half-ran all the way back to the hospital, to the On Call Room, to each other's arms. Courtney never once thought of Sister Mary Michael.

· · · · ·

Two days later, in Courtney's E.K.G. course, the class members were told to don rubber gloves. They were going to examine a human heart today. Up until now they had only been able to obtain the heart of a cow to study, and though it was similar enough to the human heart to learn the basics, it wasn't quite the same. But now the instructor was holding an actual human heart in her hands for these few lucky students to study. They stood in a circle around the instructor and carefully and respectfully inspected the anatomy of the wondrous organ they were holding in their hands. They passed the vital organ from one student to the next and when Courtney held out her gloved hands to receive it, one of the students asked what the patient had died from.

"Massive Myocardial Infarction," came the answer.

"How long ago?" asked Courtney, never lifting her eyes from the slithery mass of muscle in her hands.

"Just last night. The patient was only twenty-six-years old."

Courtney's blood ran cold. No. It couldn't be.

The instructor continued. "The patient had Lupus Erythematosis and had been on steroid therapy for some time. If you look carefully at this heart, you'll be able to see where the infarction occurred. Can anyone tell me where it is?"

Courtney felt faint. There was no doubt in her mind that she was holding Michael McClendon's heart in her very hands. Michael, who had been talking with her just a few days ago. Michael, who had looked so well and seemed so robust. Michael, who had such a good heart . . . and such a sick one.

It would be typical of him to have donated his organs to science. In a world that was so full of heartache and selfishness and cruelty, Michael had been a giver . . . right to the very end. Courtney hoped the nuns were right. That there was a special place in heaven for the givers in the world. But then, she felt a bit like a six- or seven-year-old child beginning to feel the first nagging suspicion that there is no Santa Claus, no matter how much you want to believe there is.

Courtney looked down at the heart in her hands. For the first time in her short career as a nurse, she had to excuse herself and get to the bathroom so she could be sick. She didn't like this job anymore. It was too sad. It was too scary. It made her face far too many truths and to see the absurdity and unpredictability of life. And she really didn't want to know about such things just yet. She liked things to be orderly and predictable and fair.

It was only the first of many hard lessons the Nursing profession was about to teach her.

CHAPTER NINE

"LESSON ON LEECHES"

The calendar said March fourth but, for Courtney Quinn, it was the day after Christmas. She had worked both Christmas and New Year's Days on the 3 to ll shift, and was just now getting her holiday time for working Christmas. Her New Year's Day probably wouldn't come until sometime in May. But she was very glad to have had an extra day off this week. After that episode with Michael McClendon's heart, she had needed a couple of days away from this wearisome and dismal hospital world.

On her way down the hall to report for duty, she poked her head into Tommy's room to say hello, and what she saw surprised her. Tommy Matthews and Gary Evans were sitting on Tommy's bed playing cards. Courtney had expected Gary to have been discharged by now. It had only been a fatty tumor . . . hadn't it?

Both boys looked up as Courtney greeted them. She wanted to know what was going on with Gary, but didn't dare to ask - at least not until she got the official story in Change of Shift Report.

"Where ya been?" Tommy called.

"Celebrating Christmas," she said, deliberately trying to confuse him.

The boys looked at each other. "Christmas?" they said in unison.

"Yeah, I belong to this strange religion called Nursing. We work when most of the world is celebrating holidays. And we celebrate holidays when most of the world is working. We get to fly a kite on Christmas. And I'm planning a barbecue for New Year's."

The boys tittered, unsure if she was kidding . . . or crazy. And she laughingly let them wonder as she headed for the Conference Room to receive report.

Report that day was a bit overwhelming. As everyone was gathering together, Maggie Ruggles was already in an animated conversation with one of the day shift nurses, talking about another "million dollar idea" that would, hopefully, get her out of Nursing for good. It was something she called "Old Goat Obedience School." The idea was similar to the obedience schools where people send their pets to be housebroken and taught to obey simple commands. Only this was going to be for elderly, senile patients whose families were now burdened with them and who didn't know how to cope. The idea was for a six-week course in obedience for which Maggie would charge a steep sum of money (but would be careful to charge less than the cost of a nursing home). She didn't discuss the method she would use to train these people, but she did mention something about visiting a kennel and several obedience schools for pets in order to get some ideas. And even though they knew she wasn't serious - at least they hoped she wasn't - even some of the old timers were a little shocked and offended at Maggie's latest idea. But Maggie went on undaunted.

"I could be like old 'Lady Liberty.' But instead of telling you to send me your poor, your tired and your hungry, I'll be telling people to send me their senile, their stubborn and their incontinent."

Fortunately, one of the nurses began giving report, cutting Maggie's speech short. Courtney looked across the table and was glad to see that Karen Beal was on duty with her this evening. They had a lot to catch up on. Meanwhile someone was giving report on a Mr. Hawkins who had been admitted early this morning with frostbitten fingers and toes. The weather had been unusually cold the last few days and Mr. Hawkins lived on one of Philadelphia's many steam vents. Like the others in his well known hardy group of street people, he spent most of his life curled around a wine bottle, sleeping on vents. Even when the weather was unbearably cold and Philadelphia's police went around taking the homeless to shelters, many of these people would refuse and stay outside on their steam vents, lest they lose their squatter's rights.

At the moment, Mr. Hawkins was in the operating room having parts of his fingers and toes removed. His roommate, another street person, had just come back from the O.R. where he'd had surgery for a partially amputated index finger. How the finger had become partially amputated remained a mystery, though it was thought to have something to do with a fight with a broken bottle over squatter's rights to a steam vent.

"Looks like you're gonna get to see some Leech Therapy tonight, ladies," said Maggie with a sadistic smile.

She knew this would send chills down the spines of these two still unseasoned nurses, Courtney Quinn and Karen Beal.

"I never heard of Leech Therapy," said Karen in a tremulous voice. "What exactly is it?"

Maggie was thoroughly enjoying this. "It's exactly what it sounds like."

And though Maggie took great pleasure in the discomfort of the two young nurses, everyone had to admit that she was extremely knowledgeable and an excellent teacher. She went on to explain that when extensive surgery is done on as small an area as a finger, there isn't much room for the swelling that occurs. As a result, the circulation to the finger can become compromised because there is not enough room for the blood to circulate. Therefore, live, specially bred leeches are applied to the finger . . . by the nurses. The leeches secrete a Heparin-like substance that keeps the blood from clotting so that they can suck it out of the finger. This controls the swelling and promotes adequate circulation. When the leech gets full and heavy, it eventually drops off the finger, unable to hold on any longer because of its weight. The leech is then removed from the bed with tweezers and a specimen cup . . . by the nurse. Each leech can only be used once and must be destroyed by pouring alcohol over it . . . by the nurse . . . thus disintegrating into a cloudy, bloody glob in the bottom of the specimen cup.

Courtney and Karen looked at each other, knowing that tonight would be a memorable one. They weren't wrong.

But even more upsetting than the Leech Man was the news about

Gary Evans. What was thought to be a fatty tumor turned out to be a malignant Schwanoma, a deadly form of cancer. The devastating news had been given only to his parents at this point and they had to silently bear this burden until further tests could be run to determine exactly the extent of the disease. Gary had been told only that the doctors just wanted to run a few more tests, but that everything was O.K. Courtney wondered what it must be like to be the parent of a beautiful, healthy young boy like Gary and then to be hit with news like that. She hoped she would never have to know.

The last thing they were told in report was that Mr. Black in 656 had been badgering the staff all day for a back rub.

"I think he watches too many soap operas," said Maggie. "He thinks we have nothing more to do than fluff his pillow and rub his back. He thinks only the doctors do the important work and that we are here as little handmaidens to tend to his slightest whim. But if you get a chance between the leeches and the post-ops and the admissions, you might as well give him a back rub. He'll drive you crazy 'til you do."

"One question," interjected Karen. "Where do we get these leeches from?"

"Pharmacy," Maggie answered. "They keep a big jar of them in the refrigerator. The Pharmacist won't touch them so make sure you bring a cup and a pair of gloves when you go down there to get one. Quinn, you oughta be good at this. Rumor has it you're quite the fisherman."

Everyone chuckled. Everyone but Courtney.

Courtney and Karen decided to go in together to apply the leech to the patient's finger but, since one of them had to be on the ward at all times, Courtney was elected to go to the Pharmacy to capture the doomed leech. She came back with the slimy creature in the bottom of the specimen cup and they went in together to apply it to a human finger.

"Hey man, what choo think you doin'!" exclaimed the patient. "You tryin' to torture me or somethin'?"

Courtney explained the procedure as Maggie had explained it to her. Karen tried to distract the patient by taking his medical history for the Nursing Records, something that there hadn't been time for before the patient had been whisked off to the O.R.

"Mr. Allen, do you have any allergies?' Karen asked in as professional a tone as she could muster while watching her friend pick up a live leech in a gloved hand.

"Yeah, I'm allergic to you people hangin' leeches offa my fingers."

She tried again. "Are you allergic to anything like penicillin or aspirin or certain foods?"

"No, I ain't allergic to nuthin'," came the disgusted reply.

"Have you ever been in the hospital before?"

"No. And I ain't never comin' in again. You people are crazy."

His eyes were glued to the leech that was now happily and painlessly sucking the blood from his left index finger.

"Mr. Allen," Karen continued, trying to get his undivided attention, "have you ever had heart problems or lung problems, anything like that?"

"Nope."

"Nothing? No doctor has ever told you that you have any kind of health problem?"

"Well, yeah. Once. He told me I got them very close veins."

Karen and Courtney exchanged confused looks until it occurred to them that Mr. Allen was referring to varicose veins. They had to bite their lips and avoid one another's glance to keep from laughing. Karen, with great effort, continued the interview with a straight face.

"Mr. Allen, is that the only health problem the doctor has ever told you that you have? Varicose veins?"

Mr. Allen thought for a long moment.

"Oh, yeah," he said finally. "A long time ago they told me I got that Sick As Hell Anemia, but I don't pay them no mind. They always tellin' me I'm dyin' and here I am. In a hospital with leeches hangin' off my hand. If anything is gonna kill me, it's you people."

Karen and Courtney walked outside together.

"You know, an awful lot of people would probably agree with Mr. Allen, that hospitals are bad for your health," said Courtney.

"Yeah, but how does someone with Sickle Cell Anemia survive living on the streets like he does?" wondered Karen.

"I don't know. I guess they're a sturdy lot, those street people. In fact, have you seen his lab work?" Courtney asked.

"No. Should I?"

"Well, it's pretty amazing. On paper he looks dead. I mean, his liver enzymes are through the ceiling. You look at that and then expect to see this really sickly looking guy, especially with Sickle Cell. Then you walk in there and see this feisty, rugged little guy sitting up in bed telling you you're trying to kill him. It makes you wonder if maybe, in spite of all our knowledge, we sometimes do more harm than good." She was silent for a moment. "We certainly didn't help Michael McClendon very much," she added softly.

Karen looked closely at her friend. "That hit you pretty hard, didn't it?" she asked gently.

Courtney only nodded. She didn't trust her voice. She didn't have to. Just at that moment she looked up to see what looked like Lulu, the Housekeeping lady, waving her arms wildly in the distance. Both Courtney and Karen sprinted toward the doorway that Lulu disappeared into. It looked like room 656, Mr. Black, the man who had kept asking for a back rub. Courtney tried to review the facts as she was running toward the room. He was about sixty-two years old, had a cardiac history and was in for a herniorrhaphy. "Get the crash cart!" Courtney shouted to Karen. "I'll meet you down there."

When Courtney burst through the doorway, she found the patient unconscious in the bed and the Nurses' Aide who had been giving him a back rub, unconscious on the floor. Lulu the Housekeeper was crouched down on the floor beside the Nurses' Aide, with two fingers on the unconscious woman's carotid pulse. "We need help, honey!" Lulu said with terror in her voice. "This one has a pulse, but it's weak and thready. I don't know about the other one," she said, nodding toward the unconscious man in the bed.

Courtney picked up Mr. Black's bedside telephone and dialed "5555," the number used to call a code. She felt for a pulse on Mr. Black, but could not detect one. She began one-man C.P.R. on him after instructing Lulu to stay with the Nurses' Aide. She heard the clattering sound of Karen recklessly pushing the old, rattletrap of a crash cart down the hallway. People - it seemed like millions of them - began to arrive and bark orders. There was no time to figure out what had happened until both people could be resuscitated. A group of nurses and doctors worked on the Nurses' Aide right on the floor, a perfect surface for doing chest compressions. The rest of the team flocked around the bedside of Mr. Black and took over C.P.R.

"What the fuck happened?" barked one of the residents between forcing lifesaving breaths into Mr. Black's indifferent lungs.

"I don't know," Courtney answered. "I just saw Lulu calling for help and . . ."

"Lulu?"

"The Housekeeping lady. She found them both unconscious. She didn't feel for a pulse on Mr. Black, but she said the other one had a pulse, but it was weak and thready."

"The **HOUSEKEEPER** said the pulse was weak and thready?" the resident asked, incredulous.

Courtney looked around for Lulu to confirm what she had just told the doctors, but Lulu was nowhere to be found. She had hightailed it out of there as soon as she had seen the arrival of the team. She knew better than to hang around in a situation where she was in over her head and where accusations could be made. All she had wanted to do was get help for these people. She didn't think she was any doctor or anything and she didn't want anyone accusing her of trying to be one.

The room was like a three ring circus. There were people everywhere, on the floor, on the bed, pushing equipment through and shouting orders. In the middle of all this, the patient's roommate, who was still in the room, began complaining loudly that he was cold and would someone please get him a blanket. No one really paid any attention to him as they pumped on and breathed into and started I.V. lines on the two unconscious patients.

"Oh, sure," the man grumbled. "You're always paying attention to him," he said sarcastically as he watched all the commotion. "I never ask for anything and that's exactly what I get. NOTHIN'. Goddammit, I'm cold and I want a blanket. Sure, you can give that old coot fresh ice water and back rubs, but when I ask for something as simple as a blanket, no one has any time for me."

Courtney spotted a blanket that had been thrown over the radiator earlier when Mr. Black had complained it was too hot in the room. She stepped over the code team who were kneeling on the floor, working on the Nurses' Aide. It looked as though the woman was beginning to regain consciousness. Courtney picked the blanket off the radiator and put it across the disgruntled roommate. As she did, she noticed a tube of cream lying on the floor beside the Nurses' Aide, probably the cream she had used to give Mr. Black his back rub. She casually glanced at the name of the lotion.

"Oh my God!" she gasped. "It's Nitroglycerin Paste."

"What are you mumbling over there?" barked the Code Chief.

"Nitroglycerin. She must have given the patient a back rub with Nitroglycerin Paste, thinking it was hand lotion and that's why they both coded." Courtney knew that Mr. Black applied his own Nitroglycerin Paste, one inch every six hours. He'd been doing it for years at home because of his cardiac condition and the doctors allowed him to keep it at his bedside to apply to himself since he didn't trust that the nurses would always be able to give it to him on time. The paste could also be taken if the patient had a bout of chest pain, which he frequently did. It dilates the blood vessel, especially the ones around the heart, thereby lowering the blood pressure and preventing any added strain to the heart. Only one inch of Nitro paste could accomplish all this. Mr. Black kept it in his top drawer, as Courtney recalled, where it could easily have been mistaken for hand lotion if you didn't read the label. The Nurses' Aide must have squeezed out a big glob of it and rubbed it into his back and her hands. No wonder they were both lying here unconscious!.

"Holy shit!" exclaimed the Code Chief. "I don't believe it!"

The Nurses' Aide came around first. She had a good strong pulse by now and her blood pressure was gradually creeping back up to normal. She was loaded onto a stretcher and taken off to the Intensive Care Unit. One of the residents remarked that she would probably spend the rest of her life reading labels. She was followed shortly by Mr. Black, who everyone supposed would never ask for another back rub.

CHAPTER TEN

"HIGH HOPES"

All of Gary Evans' scans had come back clean. That is to say, there was no trace of any metastasis or further disease. The surgeon had done a wide excision of the Schwanoma at the time of surgery and so was optimistic that Gary would do well. In fact, with a stroke of luck he would have no further problems or require any further treatment. Gary was clearly one of the lucky ones. He would be discharged today to his family of seven brothers and sisters, and two very loving, very relieved parents. Once again, Tommy was saying good-by to a friend, a friend who was a lot luckier than he.

Courtney saw the forlorn look on Tommy's face and her insides melted. She sat down beside him on the bed as he stared at the floor, and wordlessly put her arm around his shoulder. She could feel his wretchedness and pain.

"Do you want to talk about it?" she asked softly.

Silence was his only answer.

"I know it must be tough to be stuck in this place and watch everyone else go home," she continued, trying to draw him out.

"How would you know?" he said with just a hint of anger.

"I don't know, honey. I can only guess. I just know that sometimes talking about it makes it feel a little better."

He was silent again. He knew she was right. He did want to talk about it, but for some reason needed her to pull it out of him. He gave her a hint. "I'm scared, Courtney."

"I know, Tommy. Tell me about it. Tell me what's scaring you."

"Michael. I heard he died." Tommy looked at her with tear-filled brown eyes.

So he knew. She had wondered if he did, but she hadn't wanted to be the one to bring it up. "I know," she said gently.

"Courtney, what's going to happen to me? I mean I know I'm going to die and all that, but it never really seemed real until I heard about Michael. I hate the thought of dying."

They didn't teach these things in college. Courtney didn't know what to say. She only knew what not to say. Like that everything was going to be OK or that medical science would save him. Those answers only would have made her feel better. And they both knew it was a lie anyway.

"All I know, Tommy, is that life is very hard. And it's been really hard for you. And that you have to believe that there's a reason for the things that happen, and that there is a God who loves you and will take care of you. Do you believe in that, Tommy,"

"Yes." He said it meekly. "But I'm still scared. I hope they don't bury me. I hate the thought of lying under that cold ground, especially in the winter. I'd rather be cremated."

Courtney was glad the room was dark and that no lights were on yet. She tried to take the tears out of her voice, but she couldn't take them out of her eyes. "I'm not afraid for you," she said. She swallowed hard. "If I were God, I'd take you right up to Heaven with me and give you all the Incredible Hulk comic books you could read, and front row seats to a Pirates game and . . . ."

". . . and a strong, athletic body so I could be a star athlete," Tommy piped up.

". . . and a million gorgeous girl friends," Courtney laughed as she sniffled.

". . . and a million dollars," he continued.

"... and an endless supply of chocolate layer cake."

"... and pizza," he added, laughing now.

"Just think," Courtney said wistfully. "If you and I can come up with all that stuff, and we're only human, just think what good stuff God has in store for you."

Tommy liked that thought. And he loved her for bringing it to his attention. "I'm always gonna watch over you, Courtney," he promised, enjoying the role reversal for a moment.

"Thank you," she said sincerely. "And I'll meet you there someday, and I know we'll have a lot to talk about."

When she left him, Tommy was his old self again. His dinner tray had arrived and he ravenously dug into it. Courtney turned his T.V. on as she walked out the door and told him not to watch any X-rated movies to get any more ideas about heaven. Tommy blushed and Courtney wiped the last remaining tear from her eye before venturing into the routine chaos of the rest of the ward.

Paul Edwards, the plainclothes police officer, approached her as she exited Tommy's room. "Excuse me, Nurse, but do I detect a trace of sadness in those beautiful blue eyes?" he asked.

"Well, if you don't, you have no business being a detective or whatever it is you are."

"Rough night, huh?" he said, completely understanding and forgiving of her sarcasm.

"Yeah," she said with tears in her eyes. "It just seems so unfair that someone as young as Tommy has to cope with questions that even the wisest sage can't answer. I feel so helpless and inept. I wish I could help him somehow."

"You are helping him, Courtney," Paul said sincerely.

"I wish I believed you. It all seems so futile."

Paul studied her pained expression for a long moment. "You can't save the world, Courtney," he said in the voice of a man who knew what he was talking about. "I used to be like you. I know what it's like to ache and to hurt for someone else's problems. But you know what?"

She really didn't want to know . . . but he gave her no choice.

"The only problems you can solve are your own . . . if you're lucky."

Courtney wondered who he thought he was, giving her this unsolicited advice.

"Now, you may wonder who I think I am giving you all this unsolicited advice," he continued, "but remember this. It's hard to smell the roses when you're sitting in a pile of shit."

"How profound," she said sarcastically.

"O.K., what do I know? I'm just a cop assigned to hang out here on your floor. But I do know enough to see that you're getting too involved with this kid. And it's gonna cost you, Courtney Quinn."

Truer words were never spoken.

CHAPTER ELEVEN

"FREE SPIRITS"

6-South had an unusually large amount of overflow Orthopedic patients lately. Most of these patients were nursing home material but had been admitted for various and sundry hip fractures and hip surgeries. The Orthopedic service was most anxious to discharge them back to the nursing homes they had come from, once the residents had their chance at learning various surgical procedures on them. As far as the Ortho residents were concerned, these patients had served their purpose.

They didn't appreciate it when these patients developed any type of post-operative complications such as pneumonia, chest pain and/or decubitus ulcers (more commonly known as bedsores or pressure sores). Not that the Nursing staff particularly enjoyed these post-op complications either, but they got right to work on them, especially the bedsores, and often had some pretty impressive results. That is until one of the administrators - a former nurse who couldn't stomach taking care of sick people and who opted instead for a well paid, 9 to 5 job, far away from sick people - decided to order a different kind of air mattress.

The nurses used air mattresses on the beds of most elderly, immobilized or malnourished patients whether or not the doctors ordered it . . . or even knew about it. Things had been going just fine and the nurses had been able to prevent and/or heal a large number of these sometimes devastating decubitus ulcers. That is until Alice Erickson, the nurse-turned-administrator, ordered a new . . . and cheaper air mattress.

Of course this was all done in the name of the budget, in spite of the knowing protests of the nurses who claimed the new mattresses actually caused decubiti because of their rigidity. And while Alice Erickson was being praised by her administrative peers for saving the hospital money, many elderly and undernourished patients were taking Demerol shots for the pain of a newly developed decubitus ulcer.

Courtney had a hard time believing that anyone who worked in a hospital, especially someone who had been a nurse, could be so heartless. She still wanted to believe that the patient's welfare, not money, always came first. But she should have known better, especially when she saw a doctor's order one day written for "standard discharge." When she questioned the resident who wrote the order, he told her the order automatically meant three things: (l) give the patient prophylactic Tylenol every four hours to prevent any fevers that would prevent the patient from being discharged, (2) pad the floor around the bed with pillows so that if the patient falls out of bed, they won't break another hip, which would keep them from being discharged, and (3) NEVER, under any circumstances, inform the patient that they are being transferred back to the nursing home, since this would only encourage the patient to spike a temperature, fall out of bed, develop chest pain or all three.

Courtney was becoming accustomed to the callous attitude and not as easily shocked as she once had been. But something she couldn't get used to was an elderly patient in 645, a woman with a fractured hip that had been repaired but who now had such severe pneumonia and multiple bedsores, that she was considered too sick to go back to the nursing home and was kept here just waiting to die. The odd thing was that she kept hanging on. Every night when Courtney left work, she told herself that, when she came back tomorrow, surely this patient would have died. And it would have been a blessing for the poor old woman who had certainly suffered enough. But everyday when Courtney came on duty, there would be this poor, elderly woman, still alive, still struggling to breathe.

One night, after a few weeks of this, Courtney mentioned it to Karen in the Nurses' Station. "I don't get it," she said. "All of her Lab work is horrendous. Her white count is up, she runs a temperature of l03 degrees twenty-four hours a day, her chest X-ray is almost completely whited out from the fluid in her lungs, and still she hangs on."

Karen pondered it for a moment. "She's just a tough old bird, I guess. She must just have some strong constitution."

"I know why she won't die," came a voice from the doorway. "And it has nothing to do with a strong constitution." It was Lulu speaking and it was the first time Courtney had seen her since the day of the Nitroglycerin double code.

Courtney had nothing but respect for Lulu's opinion on things. If anyone had ever told her when she was a student that she would rely on the opinion of a housekeeper, she would have laughed. She knew better now.

"Tell us, Lulu," she smiled, "why won't she die?"

"Her spirit isn't free," Lulu answered genuinely.

"Her spirit?" repeated Karen. "What do you mean, her spirit?"

"Just what I said, honey. You got her all cooped up in a stuffy room with the windows closed. And most of the time you got her door closed too, so's nobody has to look at her, less'n they **have** to. Her spirit is trapped. It has no way to get out."

Courtney and Karen looked at each other, not knowing quite how to take what they were hearing.

"How do you know that, Lulu?" Courtney asked respectfully.

"It's an old Jamaican ritual. You gotta give the dying a lot of room so's their spirit can get out. You go open that lady's window, even just a crack, and I guarantee she'll let go and die." That said, Lulu had nothing more to add. She picked up her mop and pail and headed for the door, leaving Courtney and Karen speechless.

"It might be worth a try," Karen suggested.

"I'm game if you are," Courtney answered, and they both headed for room 645. Courtney opened the window a crack and Karen propped the door wide open.

There wasn't much of a chance to think about it again, since

94

Courtney got a phone call then from the Admitting Office.

Gary Evans was being admitted on an emergency basis. the diagnosis: Brain Tumor.

Gary and his mother arrived on the floor about ten minutes later. Gary looked calm and smiled in recognition when he saw Courtney. He obviously had not yet been informed of the diagnosis. His mother looked concerned, but remained optimistic and confident in front of Gary. Courtney couldn't read her face, couldn't determine whether or not she knew the diagnosis. Mrs. Evans told Courtney that she had taken Gary to the eye doctor that afternoon, since he'd been complaining of blurred vision and thought that perhaps he needed glasses. When the optometrist examined Gary's eyes, something disturbed him and he suggested that Gary be seen right away by his personal physician. Everyone had been somewhat mysterious about what they were suspecting at this point, and Gary and his mother were not at all sure what they were doing here. Courtney made Gary comfortable in his room as she sent his mother down to the Admitting Office to fill out the necessary forms.

Twenty minutes later, Mrs. Evans arrived on the floor with tears in her eyes and holding what looked to be the face sheet to Gary's chart. This is the sheet with information on it that includes the patient's name, date of birth, doctor's name, insurance carrier, etc. It also lists the Admitting diagnosis. Normally this sheet of paper is put inside a sealed envelope by the Admitting Clerk, and given to the family member to deliver to the nurses so that it can be put on the patient's chart. The Clerk hadn't bothered to put it in an envelope this time, and poor Mrs. Evans learned of her son's diagnosis in the cold sterile atmosphere of a hospital elevator, by herself.

Courtney saw Mrs. Evans approaching the Nurses' Station with an expression on her face that was beyond description.

"Can this be true?" she said, pointing to the paper that said her beautiful fourteen-year-old baby was doomed. She didn't wait for an answer. "Why didn't somebody tell me? I want to speak to someone right away."

Courtney was horrified at the way this poor woman had been introduced to the most devastating news of her life. She put one hand on Mrs. Evans' trembling one and dialed the Page Operator with the other. The Neurology resident said he'd be right up. In the meantime, Mrs. Evans went to the phone to call her husband. Courtney could not imagine a more poorly handled situation than this one.

By later that evening, Gary's room was filled with his seven brothers and sisters and his agonizing parents. Several consults were done, faster than Courtney had ever seen any **one** consult done, and several opinions were offered. The consensus of opinion was that time was of the essence, and that Gary needed surgery to remove this tumor - the sooner, the better.

Courtney had never seen a more loving or more courageous family than Gary's. And if they were brave, Gary was something that went beyond words. He still had a child's trust that his mother and father could fix anything and he refused to be frightened. Gary was used to winning.

It was decided that surgery would be performed first thing in the morning. This meant that all kinds of stat bloodwork and tests had to be done tonight. It also meant that an orderly would be in to shave Gary's beautiful, thick head of hair.

Courtney was just coming out of Gary's room when she spotted Dave leaning on the chart rack, flirting with the cute little Lab Technician who had come to draw Gary's stat bloodwork. The petite blonde tech was thoroughly enjoying Dave's attention. Courtney stopped for a moment and watched them as Dave turned on his charm and the Lab Technician blushed. Wanda the Ward Clerk came up behind Courtney rather unexpectedly and whispered, "I told you so."

Courtney was about to walk away when she heard Dave telling the little blonde that he would see her Friday at Happy Hour in the hospital hangout across the street called Epstein's Barr. She couldn't believe what she was hearing. Dave turned around just in time to see Courtney's fallen face. He walked toward her smiling, beginning his defense. He knew he was caught, but he had no doubt he could smooth things over.

"Oh, c'mon. What's with the long face?" he laughed a bit uncomfortably.

"How could you?" was all Courtney could manage to say at first.

"What? There's a little party at Epstein's Barr Friday night and I asked her to go. What's the big deal? I already looked at your schedule and you're working." He honestly seemed to believe that what he was saying made perfect sense.

"What does that make me? A convenience? Was I just lucky enough to have my schedule coincide with yours? Is that all this relationship is about?" Courtney felt physical pain in the pit of her stomach.

"Don't go getting all female on me. I never said we had an exclusive on each other. We're not married or anything."

Courtney was dumbfounded. This was not the time or place to deal with this and she knew it. But she couldn't seem to force herself to leave this hurtful scene. She felt the tears of disappointment fighting to get out, but she somehow held them back. She was disappointed in herself for having given him too much credit far too soon and for having let herself believe that she was special to him. She should have known better. She should have seen that big ego exuding from him the first night she met him when he had saved the day, like a knight in shining armor. She had thought he had done it for her, but now she could plainly see how much he enjoyed playing the role of hero. He had done it mostly for himself. She had been a fool.

She turned on her heel and walked down the corridor. She didn't know where she was going, but it didn't matter as long as she was getting away from him. He followed halfway down the hall, calling her name and laughingly telling her not to be mad. Then he shook his head, still smiling, and retreated. Such a valiant attempt.

She felt a draft as she walked past 645, and remembered how, earlier, she and Karen had cracked the window open. The late winter night was a cold one and a chill breeze wafted through the window. She walked in and found Karen at the patient's bedside with an incredulous look on her face.

"She's dead, Courtney. Lulu was right. Her spirit just needed some room to get out."

Courtney forgot her pain for a moment. This was almost frightening. "Please tell me she's a D.N.R." Courtney remarked.

"D.N.R.? What's that?"

"You know, 'Do Not Resuscitate.' An order in the chart that says we don't have to call a code. If it's not there, we have to call one."

"Oh, no," groaned Karen. "Don't tell me that during all this time we've been waiting for her to die, no one ever thought to get an order for that. Maybe we should just wait `til we know she's good and dead and then we can call the code team. That way they'll never get her back. Really, it would be the kindest thing to do," she said, almost pleading.

Courtney went out to check the chart. There was no D.N.R. order. It had been overlooked and now this poor woman and the code team were going to pay for the oversight. Courtney picked up the phone and called the code. She was amazingly calm and she wasn't sure if it was because she hoped the old woman couldn't be revived (for her own good) or because her heart weighed a thousand pounds right now.

The woman couldn't be revived. Thank God. Her spirit had flown. Lulu looked knowingly in the door and smiled.

Gary's family was leaving for the night, and they all hugged and kissed Gary goodnight. The love among them was almost palpable . . . and so was the pain.

Courtney walked into his room after everyone had left. The orderly from the O.R. had already been there to shave his head, and Gary sat in a chair, attached to an intravenous and wearing a wool ski cap over his freshly shaven head. He looked like a "What's wrong with this picture?" puzzle. He was too young and too healthy to be sitting in a hospital hooked up to an I.V. and awaiting brain surgery. He was smiling. He was sweet. And he had so much to live for.

Courtney pulled up a chair. "How ya feeling, Gary?"

"Bald." He said it with a smile.

"You're still an awfully gorgeous guy. I bet you drive all the girls crazy," Courtney teased.

"Yeah," he agreed.

"What about tomorrow, Gary?" Courtney said seriously. "Is there anything I can explain to you again to help you understand?"

Gary shook his head. "Not really. They've been explaining things to me all night."

"Yeah, I guess you must be an expert on it by now."

Courtney had lots of work to do. And she had fulfilled her obligation to Gary. She had explained everything she could think of to him about the pre-operative medication that he would be receiving, and that he would be asleep for the surgery and that he would be in the Intensive Care Unit when he woke up. But she couldn't leave him alone just yet. It had to be terribly frightening to be fourteen and alone and know that you were having brain surgery in the morning. "Hey, I know," she piped up. "Would you like to see where the Intensive Care Unit is and where your parents will be waiting for you?"

Gary brightened at the idea. "Yeah, I was wondering about that. Can you take me for a walk up there?"

Courtney took Gary past the Operating Room and to the doors of the Intensive Care Unit, careful not to let him glimpse the frightening sight of mechanical paraphernalia that lay just inside those doors. She showed him the Waiting Room where his family would be able to stay twenty-four hours a day, and he seemed relieved to know how physically close it was to where he would be. Suddenly he turned to her and asked, "Is Tommy still here?"

Of course. Why hadn't she thought of that? In fact, Tommy didn't have a roommate at the moment. But it was getting late. Almost eleven o'clock - he might be sleeping. She hadn't had a chance to spend any time with Tommy tonight. But moving Gary into that room would probably be good for both of them.

"Not only is he here," Courtney answered, "but he's fresh out of roommates. Would you like to move in with him for tonight?"

Gary agreed and Courtney made the arrangements and transferred Gary's belongings herself, since the Nurses' Aide and Wanda the Ward Clerk were mad at her for causing this disruption so close to the end of the shift.

Paul Edwards, the plainclothes police officer, took Gary's suitcase from her so that she could give her undivided attention to rolling Gary's ancient I.V. pole without disturbing the placement of the intravenous needle. Tommy was only too happy to see his old pal, Gary. And very sad that it would only be for one night.

"Don't you ever sit down and relax?" Paul Edwards asked after helping Courtney complete the move.

"Never," She said. "I might miss something."

"Or have to face something. Like your feelings," he added.

Courtney stared at him. "What exactly is it you're saying?" she asked.

"Just that you should have belted that doctor boyfriend of yours tonight."

That hurt.

"Look, I'm not trying to hurt your feelings or anything, but that guy's a whoremaster. I've seen him do this number before on really nice girls. He's known for it. He's got an ego problem."

"He's a doctor, what do you expect?" Courtney said with a note of bitterness that surprised even her.

"I would expect someone as smart as you and as pretty as you to see through a guy like that."

"And what makes you think you know so much about people and relationships and all these crazy things that go on up here?"

"It's my job. I have to understand people so I can predict what they're gonna do. I'm a trained observer."

"Well then, tell me this, Mr. Trained Observer," her voice began to quiver a bit, "what's that Lab Technician got that I don't have?"

CHAPTER TWELVE

"THE SOW'S EAR"

When Courtney came on duty Friday afternoon, she noticed several fans, the kind Housekeeping uses to dry a freshly waxed floor, sitting in the doorways of three different rooms. Oddly enough, they were the rooms of the overflow Orthopedic patients.

"What, did we have a massive discharge of Orthopedic patients today?" she asked, knowing that Housekeeping didn't usually wax a floor unless the room was at least temporarily empty.

Maggie Ruggles looked up and laughed. "No, but we're trying. Just ask Mark," and she nodded her head in the direction of Mark Duffy, who was just approaching the Nurses' Station, carrying what looked like another fan with a big "Happy Face" painted on the blades. Mark read the utter confusion on Courtney's face and decided to have some fun with her.

"Courtney, I'd like you to meet 'Fanny,' the electrical angel of death."

"What's going on around here, has everyone lost their minds?" Courtney said in total bewilderment.

Maggie took over. "Well, when word spread about how you and Beal finally figured out a way to make a lingering, Orthopedic G.O.R.K. go to that big nursing home in the sky, the boys (meaning the orthopedic residents) decided to get creative."

"I don't know what you're talking about," Courtney answered honestly.

"Oh, come now," Mark smiled, "don't be so modest. Your idea about 'letting the spirit fly' was brilliant."

"It wasn't my 'idea,'" she answered. "And I don't know what you're doing, but I think you're being incredibly disrespectful, especially for someone who calls himself a healer."

"I'm not calling myself a healer. Although a few times, I think I've been referred to as a heel." He put his arm around Courtney. "C'mon, Quinn, where's your sense of humor?"

"I lost it last night," she said truthfully.

But Mark paid her no mind. He looked at "Fanny" as her happy face twirled around when he pushed the "on" button. "You see," he began, assuming that, of course, Courtney was interested in his nonsense, "when I heard the theory about giving the dying a lot of room so that their spirit can fly out of them, and saw how well it worked for you last night, I figured, why not improve on a great idea?"

Courtney stared at him like he was speaking a foreign language. Maggie looked at him like he was Thomas Edison or something.

"That's when I came up with this baby, right here," he said, patting the fan. "You see, when we have a patient like the one last night, who's just hanging on and dying inch by inch, we simply open the window and the door, like you did last night. But **this** time, we put a fan in the doorway to help blow the spirit to the window, thereby speeding up the process." Mark was obviously proud of himself. "What do you think?" he added.

"I think you're sick," Courtney said flatly, before heading for the Conference Room to begin report.

She was the first one there and so she settled down heavily in a chair to await the rest of the staff. Mark walked in behind her and pulled up a chair.

"Dave told me you two had a little tiff last night," he began.

"It wasn't a tiff. He flirted with some Lab Technician right in front of me and then had the nerve to tell me he's taking her to some party tonight." Courtney couldn't hide her indignation.

"Listen, Dave can be a real asshole sometimes but. . . ."

"Tell me something I don't already know."

"But he's really a good guy, Courtney. He's just got a tremendous ego. And here's something that might surprise you. He's really afraid of women."

"Yeah, I suppose that's why he went into OB/GYN," Courtney answered sarcastically.

"You know, in a way, that's precisely why a lot of those guys go into it. It makes them feel looked up to by women or something. I'm telling you, Courtney, he's scared to death that women only want him because he's a doctor and will make a couple of bucks one day."

"Poor baby. If he's so scared, then why does he go around flaunting his attitude of 'I'll make it all better, I'm the big, strong, smart doctor?'"

"That's exactly why he does it. Dave's a real insecure guy. He once told me that all women have the olfactory receptors of a bloodhound when it comes to sniffing out a guy with money and a little prestige. Yet he's afraid that's all he's got to offer."

"Well, thank you very much, Sigmund Freud. But if that's really how he feels, that doesn't say very much about his opinion of me, does it?"

"Courtney, Dave has a lot of growing up to do, maybe, but he's really a good guy. Trust me."

Just then a few nurses from the day shift straggled in, including Maggie Ruggles. Though they were anxious to start report, they were also busy complaining about how short staffed they had been today.

Mark took his cue and left, and Courtney sat there listening to the usual complaints until she couldn't keep from asking the group of them,

"Why don't you quit complaining and **do** something about it?"

The room was silent. Maggie was the first to retaliate. "And just what do you suggest we do, O Experienced One?"

Courtney was immediately sorry she had started this. "I don't know. I just know that it can't be healthy to be this unhappy and to feel this abused for this long. There must be some kind of procedure for registering a formal complaint, isn't there?"

"Yeah, it's called 'calling out sick' . . . cause you're sick and tired of being a workhorse. An underpaid workhorse at that," Maggie answered.

"What about filing a grievance against Administration for not giving you the staffing you need?"

This brought a roar of laughter from every seasoned professional in the room . . . which was everyone but Courtney.

"Have you ever heard the saying that you can't make a silk purse from a sow's ear?" Maggie interjected.

So that's what that saying meant. Courtney had never understood it before.

Well, that's their answer," Maggie went on to explain. "They'll tell you they don't keep a bunch of little elves, or better yet, nurses, locked in the cellar, that they can just let out when they need them. They say, simply, that there just **are** no nurses to send. And that's true. But the answer is, because they work them too hard, give them no credit and no respect for doing what most people wouldn't even do for a relative, let alone total strangers, and don't pay them enough to make it worth the aggravation."

Those were hard words to refute, especially because, in her heart, Courtney agreed with Maggie. "Listen, I'm not looking for an argument and I have a lot of respect for what you're saying. And even though I've only been doing this for a short time, I can see that there are some real

105

drawbacks to being a nurse. But, what I don't understand is, if you hate it so much, why did you go into it in the first place?" Courtney even surprised herself with the courage it took to ask a question like that of the volatile Maggie Ruggles.

But Maggie's reply was not an angry one, as everyone in the room was expecting. It was just a sad one and a tired one.

"Because in my day, if you wanted to be a professional of some sort, you had **two** - count them - **two** choices. A nurse or a teacher. And I was never really known for my patience with children - or with anyone else for that matter. Plus I was sick of school from being there twelve years anyway. And I wanted the 'excitement' of Nursing. By the time you realize how fed up you are with Nursing, you're too tired to go back to school for something else and start your life over. At least today, it's common practice and totally acceptable for a little girl to want to grow up to be a doctor or a lawyer. In my day, the closest you could get to those professions was to marry one . . . and I wasn't willing to go that far."

The rest of the 3 to 11 shift had filed in during Maggie's little speech, and was more interested in getting report started than in listening to any "Why I Became A Nurse" speech. Still, Maggie had given Courtney a lot to think about. Why not start challenging Administration? Someone had to if things were ever going to change. And, God knows, things certainly needed to change.

When report finished, Maggie still hadn't. She made her way over to Courtney and pulled her aside. "Listen, Quinn, you may not believe this, but I like you. That's why I'm going to give you some valuable advice. Don't go thinking you're gonna change the world. I know you're idealistic and all that crap, and that's fine. You're still young. But if you have any ideas about approaching Administration and filing grievances against them, get them out of your head. You'll never win. They'll just label you a complainer and turn a deaf ear to you. I'm telling you this for your own good."

Courtney looked Maggie directly in the eye, no longer capable of being intimidated by her. "It's a different world than the one you grew up in, Maggie."

"Not that different."

"Things don't change if someone doesn't stand up and say they've had enough abuse," Courtney said quietly.

"Not if that 'someone' has committed the Three Mortal Sins of Life on the Planet Earth."

"Mortal sins?"

"Yeah. Being Female, Catholic and a Nurse. You're automatically programmed to feel unworthy and uncomfortable if you're not being abused. It's a lot to overcome, Quinn. I haven't seen too many people do it. I'm not sure you've got what it takes. Do yourself a big favor and pipe down."

Maggie had no way of knowing that she had just created a monster.

CHAPTER THIRTEEN

"NURSES AND COPS?"

Gary's Neurosurgeon did not have good news for the Evans family. The tumor had been larger than suspected and was too deep and too extensive to remove without leaving Gary paralyzed, comatose or dead. They took what they could and hoped that radiation and chemotherapy would destroy the rest of it, but no one was terribly optimistic.

Courtney had begun coming to work a few minutes early each day so she could run up to the I.C.U. and spend a few minutes with Gary. Always, there were several members of the Evans family sitting outside in the Waiting Area, ready to jump if Gary needed anything or if there were any change in his condition. And though Gary may not have had a lot going for him as far as the diagnosis was concerned, Courtney couldn't see how he could lose with a family as supportive as this. They were there around the clock and Courtney knew that even though Gary drifted in and out of consciousness, he must, on some level, be aware of all the love and support that surrounded him twenty-four hours a day.

Courtney only spent a few minutes with him because she knew he needed his rest and usually wasn't sure if he was conscious. But that never stopped her from holding his hand and talking softly to him. She learned, both in school and from real life experience, that hearing is the last sense to go when one loses consciousness and the first to come back. Even when a person appears to be unconscious and unresponsive, there is still a good chance that they can hear the kind words spoken to them. Of course, Gary couldn't have responded if he wanted to, since he'd be unable to talk due to the trache tube that sat in his throat and was hooked up to a ventilator on the other end that forced measured breaths into his lungs.

Courtney squeezed his hand. It was cold and swollen from the multiple sticks for blood and the ever-present intravenous. She stroked the side of his head, careful to avoid the big ugly incision that was held together with surgical staples. The hair was just beginning to grow back and it was prickly against Courtney's soft hand. "Hi, Gary, it's Courtney," she murmured to him. "I wish you'd hurry up and get well enough to come back downstairs. Tommy and I miss you."

She couldn't be sure, but she could have sworn that she saw the beginning of a tremulous smile cross Gary's lips. "I know you can hear me, Gary," she went on, encouraged. "And it's all going to be O.K. You're still in Intensive Care. Remember? The place I showed you the night before the surgery. And your whole family is right outside in the Waiting Room I showed you. They're always there, Gary, just waiting for you to get better . . . and you better hurry up because with the size of your family, there's no room for anyone else out there."

This time she saw it for sure. There was no doubt that Gary flashed her a smile. Her heart lightened. "O.K., Gary, you get some rest now. I have to go to work. I'll tell Tommy you said 'hi.' In the meantime, don't forget that your family is right outside this door, day and night, and they're not leaving 'til they see you get better." She squeezed his hand again then made her way to the elevator and to 6-South.

She was still a little early and so decided to get a cup of coffee and sit down and relax for a few moments before beginning her eight hours of chaos. At least Karen was working tonight. They hadn't had much time to talk recently and Karen had seemed a little preoccupied lately. She wondered what was going on to make Karen so distracted these days. Probably a man. That's what usually did it. And speaking of men, Courtney was painfully aware that she had not heard a word from Dave since the night of the Lab Technician incident. She felt hurt and betrayed, but it was up to him to call her. She was not about to feed that massive ego any further.

The door opened and Paul Edwards walked in to get a cup of coffee. Courtney looked up and smiled. "Still guarding Philadelphia's finest, are you?" she said, just making polite conversation. Paul had always been very nice to her and she felt badly that, every time they talked, it seemed she was in the middle of one crisis or another and ended up being sarcastic with him.

"You know, if I didn't know better," he said, ignoring her questions, "I'd swear you were this nurse named Courtney Quinn. You look just like her. But everybody knows that Courtney Quinn never has time to sit down and take a breather." He was smiling and Courtney noticed for the first time what a lovely smile he had.

"O.K. I guess I deserve that," she bashfully admitted.

"What? You agree with me on something? This must be my lucky day."

"Listen. Don't push your luck," she said good naturedly. "I guess you just keep catching me at bad times. I want to apologize if I've been rude."

"It's all right." he said, again with that gorgeous smile. "Only another nurse . . . or a cop . . . could understand what you guys go through up here."

"A cop?" Courtney asked with genuine surprise.

"Yeah. Nurses and cops have a lot in common. I bet you never thought about it before."

"Like what?" She was a little intrigued.

"Like we all screw our systems up by working all these crazy shifts. And we never get to celebrate holidays on the actual holiday. Not to mention weekends. And we're all public servants - trying to help people and often getting spit in the face for it."

"You make it sound so glamorous," Courtney teased.

"But you know what really links us together?" he asked, purposely ignoring her last comment.

"No, what?"

"Nursing and police work are the only two professions in which you

110

can experience every human emotion in one eight-hour shift."

Courtney liked that. She had never thought about it that way, but he certainly was right. She had to give this man credit. He truly seemed to think long and hard about things. She hadn't known cops could be so introspective. She glanced down at her watch and gasped. "Yikes. I gotta get to work. They're probably wondering where I am."

"Well, it was nice talking to you, Courtney Quinn. I'm glad we finally had a civilized conversation."

"Me, too," she laughed, then disappeared out the door.

.....

The ward was in its usual state of urgency and disarray. But Karen and Courtney were beginning to get used to it now. They didn't get upset over the "little" things like visitors complaining about the care or doctors yelling about why a patient hadn't been gotten out of bed yet. They just went along doing the best they could and understanding that never would their best be enough, and that, always, there would be people complaining.

"I'm glad to see you're looking a little better today," Courtney said to Karen as they made up a bed for a new admission.

"What do you mean?" asked Karen. "Have I looked sick lately?"

"No, just preoccupied," Courtney shrugged.

"Either you're very perceptive or I'm very transparent," Karen answered after a brief hesitation.

"Want to talk about it?"

"Not much to say." Karen shook her head. "It's about a man."

"I thought so. What kind of man? C'mon, let me in on it."

"Well, there's this guy I've been dating," Karen began.

"Who? Do I know him?"

"Well, actually, I think you do. He, uh, well, he was a patient."

"A patient?" Courtney was surprised and a little concerned that her friend would date a patient.

"Oh, we didn't get personal, or go out or anything until a few weeks after he was discharged," Karen answered, reading the look on Courtney's face.

"Who is he? Which patient? Let me see if I remember him."

Karen was obviously uncomfortable, but finally she answered, "Robert Nelson," then waited for the grenade to explode.

"Robert Nelson, Robert Nelson," Courtney mumbled, flipping through the Rolodex in her memory of patient names. "**Robert Nelson!**" she finally wailed in disbelief. "The paraplegic?"

"Yes," said Karen calmly. "He said we'd get reactions like this but honestly, Courtney, I didn't expect it from you."

"I'm sorry, Karen, really I am. I'm just a little surprised, that's all. How long have you been seeing him? It's been a pretty long time since he was a patient here. About six months, isn't it?"

"Seven months since he was a patient. Six months since I've been seeing him. Courtney, he's a very special person. When you first see him, I suppose its' natural to see only his handicap, but there's so much more beneath that."

"I'm sure there is, Karen," Courtney said, beginning to recover from the shock. "It's just that, well, what about the future? What if you fall in love with this guy? Do you really want to spend your life working all day as a nurse, and then going home to the same thing? And what about sex?" Courtney didn't wait for answers. "Karen, you'd better get out before you fall in love."

"It's way too late for that, Courtney," Karen smiled. "I love him very much. He's been forced, mostly because of his injury, I suppose, to look within himself and to become a **real** man. Not like some of these phony jerks who go around screwing everything that walks, just to prove what studs they are."

What Karen was saying made perfect sense. And it made Courtney think of Dave, especially the part about being a phony and a stud. "What about children?" Courtney asked.

"There are ways." Karen answered confidently. Apparently the subject had already been discussed. "He's asked me to marry him," Karen added.

"What did you say?"

"I told him I need some time to think. He told me to take all the time I need. He also said he'd understand if I said no. There's absolutely no ego involved in this. He's quite a man."

"I guess so," Courtney answered absently. But she couldn't help thinking of all the nurses who marry people who **need** them. It was strange how everyone always seemed to assume that nurses marry doctors. Courtney knew more nurses who were married to alcoholics, wife-beaters and jobless men. She thought about what Maggie had said the other day about being female, Catholic and a nurse. How it sets you up to be a giver without thoughts of receiving or even asking for anything in return. You are simply encouraged to accept that this is your lot in life and that is all you need or deserve. You are encouraged to just go on living and giving until the well runs dry. Courtney hoped that wasn't what Karen was about to do. She prayed Karen really was in love and not just fulfilling her need to be needed.

"I'm going to tell him 'yes,'" Karen said softly.

Courtney put her arms around her friend and murmured, "Then I'm happy for you, Karen. And I wish you only the best."

......

Mark Duffy stopped down on 6-South a little while later. "Hey, Courtney," he said, putting a hand on her shoulder. "Did you eat dinner yet?"

"Are you kidding? You've been sending too many post-ops for us to even think about dinner," she answered, only half-kiddingly.

"Let me make it up to you," he laughed. "I'll take you across the street to McDonald's if you have time now."

Courtney looked at Karen. "Can you hold the fort for about half an hour?"

"Sure. As long as you bring me back some french fries," she bargained.

"Thanks," said Mark, before Courtney could answer, and he put an arm around her shoulder, turning her to the door.

Spring was upon them now and the evening was warm enough to warrant only a light sweater. Courtney grabbed hers and put it on as she and Mark left the area. As soon as they were out of earshot of anyone, Mark asked if she'd heard from Dave lately.

"No," she said flatly, not giving any hint of emotion.

"You know he feels really lousy about what happened," Mark began.

"He should," Courtney said without missing a beat. "What did he do, ask you to do his talking for him?"

114

"Not really. Well, sort of. He's afraid you're too mad at him to listen to him."

"Well, he got that part right. Besides, what did he expect? That I'd go running back to his arms? He better not hold his breath waiting."

They were standing now at the busy intersection right outside the hospital. Some people said the hospital was built in this location because, since there were so many traffic accidents on this corner, a hospital in this vicinity would never go out of business. It was likened to a duck crossing. Popular belief was that, when a certain number of ducks are run over in a certain area, the city or town puts up a "Duck Crossing" sign. The logic with the hospital was the same. Enough people must have been smushed on this corner to warrant putting up a hospital. Courtney laughed, in spite of her troubles, as this thought crossed her mind. Suddenly she heard Mark say "Forgiveness," and she had no idea what he was talking about.

"What?" she asked.

"Forgiveness. You were asking what I thought Dave wanted. He wants you to forgive him. He knows he was a jerk."

"Well, why can't he tell me that himself?"

"He will if you let him. He's waiting in McDonald's for us."

Courtney didn't like being sucked into this. She didn't like it that Dave had sent Mark to scout out the territory for him either. But she did like hearing that at least Dave knew he had been wrong. And she did miss him. Then it occurred to her that if all three of them were eating here, Dave would have to make his apology in front of Mark. She would have preferred a bit more privacy.

"What are you doing in the hospital at this hour anyway?" she asked Mark. "Are you on call or something?"

"Nah. I'm moonlighting in the Emergency Room. Tryin' to make a

115

little extra money. So far it's been pretty quiet."

Courtney spotted Dave sitting at a table in the corner, as she and Mark walked up to the counter to order. Mark wanted a burger, fries and a milkshake. Courtney could never understand how these guys could consume so much food without getting fat. Then it was her turn. She ordered a burger and a diet soda, and felt guilty about it. Mark remembered to order Karen's fries just as the woman asked, "For here or to go?"

"For here," they said simultaneously.

Just then there was an ear-splitting screech of tires and the sound of metal crashing into metal and glass breaking. All eyes turned toward the window just as the body of a man went hurtling through the air and landed with a bone-shattering thud in front of another car.

Everyone in the crowded McDonald's was speechless for a moment, except Mark.

"Make mine to go," he said.

CHAPTER FOURTEEN

"MOTORCYCLE MAMA"

"I'm sorry," Dave said to Courtney. "I guess I was a jerk."

"I just don't understand, Dave. You always tell me how much you enjoy being with me, and then you go and ask someone else out, right under my nose. That really hurt."

"Courtney, I'm sorry. I do love being with you. I guess I was just getting scared that I was loving it too much."

"Oh, and we wouldn't want anything like that to happen, now would we?" Courtney asked with fire in her eyes.

"Look, I don't expect you to understand. It's the age-old argument between men and women. Women want commitment. Men want freedom. It's as simple as that. We were getting too close and I'm afraid you're gonna start wanting things that are going to limit my freedom." Dave was only convincing himself.

"Wait a minute. Back up. It's not about the freedom versus commitment issue. It's about acting like a grown-up." Courtney was not about to swallow the "poor little misunderstood me" speech Dave was giving her. "And, furthermore, what makes you think it's only men who want their freedom? **Everyone** wants their freedom, until they meet someone they grow to love. Then, what you're calling commitment is actually the epitome of freedom. Two people can be free to be exactly who they are, and know that they are loved. No need to put on airs or pretenses. I thought we were on our way to that, but I guess I was wrong."

Dave was silent for a moment, then he took Courtney's hand in both of his and looked into her tormented face. "You're right, Courtney, we were on our way. We do have something special. I just got scared and tried to screw it up. I'm really sorry. And I promise that, if you'll forgive me, I'll try to straighten out. I don't blame you for being pissed. I acted like a real jerk."

Courtney was silent as she studied the earnestness on his face and the traces of apprehension in his blue, blue eyes. She leaned forward, tilted his chin with her hand and whispered, "Yes, but you're **my** little jerk."

....

When Courtney returned to 6-South, it looked as if someone had dropped a bomb on it. The crash cart was not in the Nurses' Station and no one seemed to be around, except Wanda the Ward Clerk, who was busy answering four ringing telephones. There seemed to be a lot of commotion farther down the hall, where furniture had been pushed into the hallway and shouts were coming from the room. Courtney looked at Wanda, who covered the mouthpiece of the phone she was on and mouthed the word "Tommy."

Courtney all but flew down the hall to his room. Oh, God, no. Please no. Not yet. He's just a baby. She entered his room just as the Code Chief said somberly, "Thank you very much everybody." Interpretation: "It's over. There's nothing more we can do."

The team filed out one by one, dragging their equipment with them. Courtney walked up to the bed and held her precious Tommy's hand. "I'm sorry, baby," she whispered with tears in her eyes. "I'm sorry this had to happen and I'm sorry I wasn't here to at least hold your hand through it." And though she knew it was unfounded, her guilt was overwhelming. She stroked Tommy's hair and one of her tears fell on his chest and mixed with the blood from the subclavian line they had put in during the code. She began cleaning off the worst of the blood. Karen said she'd ask one of the Aides to prepare the body for transfer to the morgue, but Courtney wouldn't hear of it. She would do it herself. She lifted his head tenderly and pulled the bloodstained pillow case out

118

from under his head. When the morgue stretcher arrived, she cradled Tommy's head in her arms so that the attendants couldn't let his head bang down on the cold metal stretcher, as she had seen so many times before.

"Were his parents notified?" Courtney asked after the stretcher disappeared into the elevator.

"Yeah. That's the first thing the Medical resident took care of," Karen answered.

"What happened?" Courtney asked. "I mean, I knew he wasn't doing real well, but I had no idea the end would come so soon."

"I don't know, Courtney. It happened right after you left. One of the Aides went in to see if he'd eaten his dinner and found him. By the time I got down there, he had no pulse and no respirations. I started C.P.R., but I guess we were just too late. We don't know how long he was like that before the Nurses' Aide found him. It could have been a good half hour."

Courtney felt sick. And she felt cheated. She knew how much he had dreaded this moment and she ached to have been with him, if for no other reason than to comfort him. She went through the rest of the night in a fog. But though Tommy's life had ended, it didn't stop the influx of new admissions and new emergencies and all kinds of other people and problems to be dealt with. There simply was no time to dwell on Tommy.

As Courtney was putting on her sweater to go home, she felt a firm hand take the garment and guide her arm into the sleeves. It was Paul Edwards.

"Another rough one, huh?" was all he said.

Courtney was just about to answer him when Wanda the Ward Clerk called to her. "Quinn, you still here? Telephone."

Courtney looked at Paul, then brushed past him to take the phone from Wanda. It was Dave, wanting to know if she'd like to meet him for a

119

drink across the street at Epstein's Barr.

"I sure could use a drink," she said miserably.

"Why? What's wrong?" Dave sounded annoyed.

"Oh, it's just been a terrible night. Do you remember Tommy Matthews, the patient I told you about?"

"Uh, yeah. I think so. He's a kid, right? The kid with Leukemia. What, is he giving you a hard time?"

"No. He died tonight."

"Well, it might have been better for him like that, you know. Fast. Some of those Leukemics' deaths are pretty horrible."

Courtney knew she was being sensitive, but she didn't like Dave referring to Tommy as one of "those Leukemics." He was a fifteen-year-old boy who had fought valiantly with an enemy that was much bigger and much stronger than he. He deserved to be remembered for the person he was, not for the disease he had.

"Oh, come on, Courtney," Dave said to the silence on the other end of the phone. "You can't go getting all caught up in your patients like this. This is a hospital. People die here. That's the way it is. You knew Tommy's time was running out. C'mon, pull yourself together and let's go out for a drink."

Courtney thought for a moment. "I don't think so," she said quietly.

"What is this 'I don't think so' crap? Two minutes ago you were saying you could use a drink. What's changed?"

"I have. I've changed my mind. I really don't feel like it."

"O.K., have it your way, but you better learn to start seeing patients as patients, not as personal friends or family members. You gotta learn to separate yourself from that place and all the people in it. I'll call you

120

over the weekend." He hung up.

"Do you know what you need, Miss Quinn?" came Paul Edwards' voice from behind her.

"A new profession, maybe. I don't think I'm really cut out for this one."

Paul laughed. "Not true," he said. "You're an excellent nurse. You just need some time away from it. I don't mean time away from the hospital. I mean time away from the whole Nursing mentality."

"You sound a bit like Maggie Ruggles."

"Bite your tongue. Even **I'm** not **that** cynical."

"So what do I do to get away from the 'whole Nursing mentality'?" she asked curiously.

"You need a day of being the 'bad guy,'" he said with confidence.

"The bad guy?" Courtney was confused.

Paul nodded. "I do it all the time. When I get tired or disgusted with being a cop, I don't shave a day or two, I wear my most raggedy jeans and holey T-shirt and go out on my motorcycle and drink beer and let everyone think I'm a 'Bad Ass Motha.' It works wonders. By the time I spend a day like that, I'm ready to come back to the way I **really** am, only now I'm refreshed. It's fun. You ought to try it sometime."

Courtney looked at him for a moment, unsure whether or not he was pulling her leg.

"I'm not pulling your leg," he said earnestly. "You really oughta try it."

"I don't have a motorcycle."

121

"Do you have a raunchy pair of jeans and a T-shirt with holes in it?"

"Doesn't everyone?" she answered.

"Perfect then. I'll pick you up at nine on my motorcycle. Better bring a sweatshirt though. It can get pretty cold on the bike."

"Wait a minute," Courtney insisted, "is this your way of asking me out on a date?"

"Yes."

"Nine o'clock in the morning?"

"Yeah."

"Tomorrow?"

"Yeah. You're off. I already checked."

"But why so early?"

"`Cause, we got a lot of fun to have, Mama. Here, write down your address." He produced a paper and pen.

Courtney hesitated for only a moment.

"Remember," Paul said as he headed for the door, "You have to look like the woman of a **Bad Dude** who rides a Harley. Motorcycle Mama. Sleaze for a Day. We're gonna make you forget everything about your conservative, professional life."

Courtney watched him swagger out the door humming the tune to Bruce Springstein's old hit "Baby, We Were Born to Run."
"Why not?" she sighed. "What have I got to lose?"

Courtney Quinn awoke early the next morning with a sense of adventure and excitement . . . feelings she hardly recognized anymore.

122

Paul had said to wear something "raunchy." That shouldn't be a problem. She slid into a pair of faded, torn jeans and a black T-shirt with a neck so stretched out it practically slipped off her shoulder. Black socks and black Reebocks came next. Yeah, she was definitely starting to look **"BAD."** She rummaged through her jewelry box until she found a pair of silver skull and crossbones earrings she'd worn once to a Halloween party. Perfect. Six silver bangle bracelets on her wrist made her look even more perfect. She studied herself in the mirror and laughed. This was already fun. She resisted the urge to wear any makeup - raunchy people don't bother with makeup. Besides, Paul was a friend, someone to have fun with. The sentimental part of her heart still belonged to Dave.

The roar of the motorcycle beneath her kitchen window jolted her back to the moment. She peered out the window and was delighted with what she saw. Paul was sitting atop a Harley Davidson "Low Rider," both gloved hands on the handgrips, the picture of masculinity. He wore the uniform of any self-respecting biker, faded jeans, motorcycle boots and a black leather jacket with the collar turned up, which only added to the appeal of his chiseled profile. There was not a trace of caution on him. He was pure rebel. Courtney wondered why she had never noticed his rugged good looks before.

"C'mon out, Mama," he called over the roar of the engine.

Courtney ran down the stairs like a little girl on Christmas morning. She shoved her apartment key and a twenty-dollar bill in her jeans pocket, tied a sweatshirt around her waist and jumped on the back of the powerful bike. No purse, no excess baggage of any kind. She was going to be totally free today. Raunchy and free. Her head jerked back as Paul let out the clutch and took off for the street. She held on to Paul's waist for dear life and put her face up to the warm Spring sun as the wind whipped through her hair and blew the skull and crossbones earrings against her head.

Paul expertly guided the bike onto Vine Street. There was no point in trying to talk since neither one could hear the other over all the noise. There was nothing to do but sit back and enjoy all the judgmental looks from motorists as Paul and Courtney roared past them. "God, if they ever knew," Courtney thought, "that we are responsible adults." A cop and a nurse who know better than to be weaving through Center City traffic on a motorcycle. But she didn't want to be a responsible adult today. She wanted to be wild and irresponsible for once in her life. She wanted people to be intimidated, to shake their heads in disapproval, to keep their distance. It was such a kick.

Paul took them down some unfamiliar side streets and pulled up in front of a run-down little store.

"Where are we?" Courtney asked, bewildered.

"You don't look quite raunchy enough," Paul smiled.

She followed him into the shabby little store and was fascinated by what she saw. All kinds of motorcycle paraphernalia lined the shelves. Leather gloves and boots. Metal studded bracelets. Wallets with metal chains. And tattoo designs, a wall full of them. Paul introduced her to the owner, a buddy of his. This so-called buddy had a full beard that was mostly gray, long gray hair braided down his back, and arms so full of tattoos that, on first glance, she thought he was a burn victim.

Paul told her she needed a tattoo . . . the kind they paint on. She studied the designs on the wall and chose one of a snake crawling by a skeleton's head wearing a top hat. Yeah, it was BAD. She wanted it on the back of her left shoulder, right where the T-shirt tended to slide off. She was feeling "badder" by the minute.

They jumped back on the Harley and rode till city streets became open highways and open highways became narrow mountain roads. They eventually pulled over to take in the magnificent view. The gentle April sun, the mountains, the wind, the first buds of Spring. God, it was all so wonderful. And, even better than the view, were all the things that weren't there. No ringing telephones. no computers. No beepers. No patient call lights. No schedules. No one asking for anything from her. Paul turned to look behind him. "Like it?"

"Do you even have to ask? It's wonderful. I feel better already."

And she did.

Paul laughed and told her to hang on as he started the bike again and headed for what looked like a little roadhouse, which turned out to be a tavern where local motorcycle gangs hang out. Paul seemed perfectly comfortable in their midst and even called one or two by name, but Courtney felt like the imposter she was. Not much escaped Paul. He sensed her uneasiness and smiled. "Relax," he said. "You'll feel better after a beer or two."

He ordered them each a brand of beer that Courtney had never heard of, but that just about everyone in the tavern was drinking. How bad could it be? The bartender slapped down two bottles in front of them and, just as Courtney was about to ask for a glass, Paul put his hand on her knee and said softly, "Motorcycle Mamas drink from the bottle."

He was right. She did feel better after a beer. Not that she fit in or anything, but she was more relaxed about the atmosphere. She was having a wonderful time.

"Now I see how you stay so happy all the time," she said, noticing that Paul still had his hand on her knee.

"There's nothing like a little harmless relaxation," he answered as he took a swig of his beer. "It makes you a better person. You should do it more often."

"Are you saying I'm not a good person?" she teased.

"Nope. You got a bigger problem than that. You're **too** good for your own good. Most people have the opposite problem. They have to learn to get disciplined and considerate. That takes some real effort. But you, you've got all that. You just have to learn how to let go of some of it. That's an easy one."

"I have a feeling I'm learning from a master," she smiled.

"Could be," he said shamelessly. "How is it you came to be such a little goody-two-shoes anyway?"

"Don't call me that. I hate that expression."

"Truth hurts, doesn't it?"

"Well, O.K., maybe I am a bit of a goody-two-shoes, but it's really not my fault. I spent my whole life in Catholic school," she said, thinking this was a pretty believable defense.

"So did I. Explain that one. Besides, most girls who go to Catholic school are the wild ones later. I guess they just get sick and tired of all those rules."

"Maybe I'm a late bloomer," Courtney said with a twinkle in her eye.

Paul stared at her for a long moment.

"Have another beer," he said.

CHAPTER FIFTEEN

"NO APOLOGIES"

The "Devil-May-Care" attitude of Courtney's day as a "Motorcycle Mama" came to an abrupt halt as soon as she arrived for work on Monday afternoon. There were three patients, including the wounded cop Paul was guarding, who had suddenly taken a turn for the worse. Technically, all three of them belonged in the Intensive Care Unit, but realistically there were no available beds there. In fact, the I.C.U. was trying to transfer several patients to the wards, stating that these patients were not actually stable, but they were the "most stable" of all the patients up there. Gary Evans was first on the list.

To his family, Gary's transfer to 6-South was a hopeful sign that Gary was recovering. And although he was holding his own, Courtney knew that the transfer simply meant there were sicker patients than Gary to be accommodated. He arrived on the ward shortly after the dinner trays had been served. Courtney was busy with one of the three "I.C.U. Candidates," a man who had received too much anesthesia from a new resident, when Gary was wheeled, in his bed, into the ward.

Courtney didn't know how she was ever going to manage so many seriously ill patients. She did have Karen working here, but some of these patients warranted very close monitoring. Other patients, like the man in 657 who had received the overdose of anesthesia, required vital signs monitored at least every half hour. Almost every patient had an I.V. running, which meant there were close to fifty I.V.s to monitor and to prevent from running dry. Karen and Courtney were the only R.N.s on the floor, and, though the Staffing Office had sent them two extra Nurses' Aides, it really didn't help matters. Only R.N.s were allowed to touch the I.V.s or perform any procedures, such as dressing changes or administration of medications. All the Nurses' Aides could do, technically, was to let them know when an I.V. was running dry and watch as Courtney and Karen scrambled frantically to get everything done and to keep everyone on schedule for medications and dressing changes.

There was not time for unanticipated emergencies tonight. So it was, of course, when they were the most frantically busy, that one of the policemen guarding the door of the cop who'd been shot approached Courtney with a concerned look on his face. She could see that he really hated to bother her when she was so rushed, but the patient he was guarding, his comrade, was having some difficulty breathing.

Courtney dropped the I.V. solution she was mixing and headed for the patient's room. Until now, he had been recovering nicely from an exploratory laparotomy that had been done to find the two bullets lodged in his abdomen. There had been talk of discharging him in the not-too-distant future. He was one of the stable ones Courtney and Karen were counting on tonight to not need very much. So much for predictions.

When she entered the room, Patrolman Davis was sitting on the side of the bed smiling, though it was evident he was short of breath. Paul Edwards and the other cop who guarded the door were at his side trying to act nonchalant. But it was plain to see they were worried.

"Mr. Davis," Courtney said in a professional and calm tone, "I hear you're having some trouble breathing."

"Oh, it's really nothing," he replied, still smiling, still trying to make light of it.

Courtney gently put her finger on his radial pulse as she spoke calmly to him. "You're probably right, but why don't you sit back and let me take your blood pressure and pulse." When she leaned over to pull the sheet over him, she noticed a reddened area on the inside of his leg. She knew what that meant. He could easily have a venous thrombosis, a blood clot in the calf of the leg, from having been on strict bed rest for so long. She also knew that his shortness of breath could be from one of the clots breaking loose and traveling to the lung, a condition called Pulmonary Embolism. The patient had been receiving a drug called "Coumadin," an anticoagulant, to prevent such a thing from happening, since Pulmonary Embolus is a frequent side effect of bed rest.

128

She calmly reached for the oxygen tubing that was on the wall over the bed. She positioned the nasal cannula on his face and turned the oxygen up to two liters per minute.

"What's all this?" he protested, embarrassed. "I'm just a little short of breath, that's all."

"Indulge me," Courtney smiled. "I promise I'll take it off as soon as the resident sees you and you convince him that you don't need it."

Vital signs were normal, but Courtney didn't like the looks of this. She excused herself and headed for the Nurses' Station to page the On-Call resident. The resident, a Dr. Decker she had never met before, came right up. He grabbed Patrolman Davis' chart on his way down the hall to the cop's room.

Not five minutes later, he emerged in a rage. "Has this patient had his Coumadin yet tonight?" he demanded of Courtney.

"Yes. He had it about an hour ago."

"How much did you give him?"

"Exactly what you ordered: Five milligrams." Courtney didn't like the tone of his voice.

"Five milligrams? I ordered **ten** milligrams," he shouted angrily.

Courtney's heart sank. Could they have given him the wrong dose of Coumadin? She could have sworn the order had said five milligrams. "May I see the chart please?" she asked as calmly as she knew how.

"There's no time for that now!" ranted the resident. "Coumadin doesn't act that quickly anyway. He's probably been receiving the wrong dose for several days. I just had him on a maintenance dose for prophylaxis and you guys screwed it all up."

If this resident was selling guilt, he found a willing customer in

129

Courtney. "Now what?" she asked meekly.

"He's obviously throwing an embolus. He needs to be in the I.C.U. where he can be watched more closely and intubated if necessary. We also need to start an I.V. and get some Heparin into him."

The resident then put down the chart and began making the necessary phone calls to get a bed for the officer in the already overcrowded I.C.U. Karen wandered into the Nurses' Station at this point and asked Courtney what was going on. Courtney reached for the patient's chart as she explained the situation to Karen. She skimmed through the doctor's orders, feeling horribly responsible for the error that the nurses had made. She finally found the order had been for five, not ten, milligrams of Coumadin. Not that it made any real difference in the situation at hand, but Courtney had to let this condescending resident know that the error, if indeed there had been an error, was his.

"Excuse me, Doctor," she said firmly, "but I'd like to show you something on this chart."

"Not now," he grumbled, "I don't have time."

"Well, you found time to berate me for a mistake I didn't make."

"I don't have time for any bullshit!" the resident blustered, hoping he could intimidate her into leaving him alone. No such luck.

"Take a look at this," Courtney continued, as she opened the chart to the page with the order he had written.

"Hmmmmmmmmmm," was all he said.

"I think you owe me an apology," Courtney said coldly.

"I think we better get this guy to the I.C.U.," was all he said.

Patrolman Davis was transferred to Intensive Care. Paul Edwards and the two body guards went with him. Courtney checked briefly on Gary, then went back to the patient with the anesthesia overdose. She

130

realized there was no way she and Karen could possibly give all their patients the kind of care they deserved by themselves. She decided to call the Staffing Office and demand more help, even though she was aware she was sounding an awful lot like Maggie Ruggles tonight.

"Mrs. Cassidy, this is Courtney Quinn on 6-South," she said in a determined voice. "Listen, I've got some really sick patients up here and only two R.N.s It's too much. Karen and I can't possibly handle it. We need more help up here."

"Just do the best you can, dear," came the patronizing reply.

"You don't understand. Our best isn't good enough. These people are sick. Three of them actually belong in the I.C.U., but there are no beds. I just sent one to I.C.U. and had to make a trade to get him there. You've got to send me more help."

"If I had the help, I'd send it to you, dear. I already sent two extra Aides."

"That doesn't help me with critically ill patients."

"It's all I've got. You'll just have to make do."

Courtney could feel her face getting red with anger. People's lives were in danger and nobody seemed to care. Then she had an idea. "What about you?" she boldly asked.

"What about me?" the Supervisor asked cluelessly.

"Why don't **you** come up and help me out?"

"Well, uh, er, that . . . you see, that's impossible."

"Why? What's more important than the safety of the patients?" Courtney asked earnestly.

"Well, Miss Quinn, yours is not the only floor in the hospital that is short staffed tonight. You have to learn to look at the whole picture." Obviously, Mrs. Cassidy had recovered from the shock of a young, mild-mannered nurse talking back to her. She wondered what this world was coming to. After all, in **her** day, if you ever talked back to a supervisor like this you would be fired. The **nerve** of these young girls today.

"Tell me, Mrs Cassidy," Courtney said, unwilling to drop the subject, "has anyone else called and told you that patients' lives are in danger if they don't get more help tonight?"

"That's none of your business, Miss Quinn. Now I suggest you get off the phone, if you're so busy, and get back to work."

Courtney would not let up. Maybe it was because she was tired of the stressful conditions and constant excuses for it, maybe it was because that obnoxious resident had tried to blame the nurses for Officer Davis' turn for the worse and then couldn't bring himself to apologize after being found out. Or maybe it was because she was finally wising up. Whatever the reason, something pushed her across a line she previously would never have crossed.

"I want it documented somewhere that I, Courtney Quinn, am telling you that lives are endangered up here and that **you** cannot or will not make the time to come up here and help out. In fact, just for the record, I'm filling out an Incident Report about this and I'll be sending copies of it to Alice Erickson and whoever is the head administrator of this place."

"I'll be up to speak with you, Miss Quinn," came a voice of controlled rage.

"I don't have any more time to talk. I have sick patients to tend to." And with that, Courtney hung up the phone. She was trembling, but proud of herself.

"Holy shit, Quinn!" Karen said in amazement. "Was that Mrs. Cassidy you were talking to like that?"

Courtney nodded.

"Wow! Congratulations! That took nerve. Are you really gonna fill out an Incident Report?"

"You bet. Even if I have to stay here 'til five in the morning finishing up my work before I get to it." She smiled confidently but she was reminding herself what she was getting ready to do and what it would mean.

An Incident Report is a form that must be filled out any time anything out of the ordinary occurs. It is often used later, if and when disciplinary action is taken, to recall the series of events and exactly what happened and who was at fault. For example, if a patient falls out of bed, the nurse must fill out an Incident Report stating whether or not the side rails were up or if the patient was sedated. It is also used if a medication error has occurred. It is similar to going to confession and admitting your guilt. Interestingly enough, you rarely see this form filled out by anyone other than a nurse. A copy of it is kept in the nurse's file and another copy is sent to Administration, for their review. It is not customary for a nurse to file an Incident Report against Administration. But then, Courtney thought, standing up straight, shoulders back, conformity never had been one of her strong points.

Courtney and Karen went back to their break-neck pace of checking everyone's I.V.s and vital signs. They passed out medications and spent their time with the most seriously ill patients. Of course, anyone who was sick enough to be in the hospital would probably consider themselves "seriously ill" and they wouldn't be wrong. But, for tonight, only the patients who complained the loudest got the attention.

As Courtney was rushing from one room to the next, she noticed Mrs. Cassidy walk onto the ward. She stood at the Nurses' Station waiting for Courtney to acknowledge her presence. Courtney sped past her and said only, "Are you here to help?"

"I'm here to have a word with you, Miss Quinn," she said authoritatively.

Courtney had a quick flashback of Sister Mary Michael. For a fleeting instant, she felt like a bad little girl who was about to get a crack across the knuckles with a yardstick. But the feeling passed and Courtney bravely answered, "Then you'll have to walk as you talk because I'm too busy to stop."

Mrs. Cassidy turned on her heel to leave. 'You haven't heard the end of this, Miss Quinn."

Courtney was certain of that.

CHAPTER SIXTEEN

"STIRRINGS"

There were two sealed envelopes addressed to Courtney Quinn tacked to the bulletin board when Courtney came to work on Tuesday. But before she was able to take them down and open them, Maggie Ruggles patted her on the back and said, "Congratulations, Quinn. I heard you gave Mrs. Cassidy a run for her money the other night. I couldn't have handled it better myself."

Courtney wasn't sure if she should be flattered or frightened.

"It's about time someone questioned what it is those supervisors actually do around here," Maggie continued. "I'll bet she didn't know what to say. Listen, if you need any help preparing for the meeting you're gonna have with a bunch of administrators, let me know. I'll be glad to give you a few pointers. God knows I've been through my share of those meetings."

"Meeting? What meeting?" Courtney asked, not recalling anything about a meeting.

"The one they're going to make you attend. They'll send you some formal invitation with a date and time on it. In fact, you're probably holding it right there in your hand. All the hot-shots from Administration will be there. They'll let you get nice and comfortable , and then they'll start the attack. They don't like it when nice little nurses speak their mind." Maggie spoke with utter authority on the subject. "You'll never win an argument with them, Quinn, but I sure am glad you had the nerve to fill out an Incident Report against them. They must be pissed."

. . . . .

Courtney opened one of the envelopes addressed to her. It was a note from Dave, scribbled on a prescription. It said simply:

"I LOVE YOU

Rx: Meet me after work tonight for a drink (Doctor's Orders)

Dr. Strauss"

Courtney felt her heart do a little flip-flop. She guessed he really was sorry about the Lab Technician incident. Maybe she had been too hard on him. He had never before told her that he loved her. She was absolutely amazed he would actually put it down in black and white. She couldn't wait to meet him after work.

Her heart was still doing somersaults from the first letter when she opened the second. It was exactly what Maggie had predicted. A letter from Administration informing her of a meeting tomorrow at one o'clock. The meeting would take place at the Administrative Offices across the street and her presence was expected. Not requested, EXPECTED. She folded the letter up and stuck it in her pocket just as it dawned on her that she would be attending this meeting on her own time.

It was only because she believed so strongly in her convictions about what had happened the other night, that she was able to put the thought of the meeting out of her mind for now. Besides, she had something lovely to look forward to - drinks with Dave tonight after work. And she also had the warm feeling that comes from knowing you are loved, especially when it's a bit of a surprise, a delicious surprise. She was convinced she could get through anything "they" (Administration) could dish out to her. She had a definite advantage.

"How's it going?" Karen asked, as she and Courtney began sorting through the new orders for the evening shift.

"Pretty good," Courtney said truthfully.

"Did you ever hear anything about the other night when you filed that Incident Report?" Karen was bursting to know. She sometimes lived vicariously through Courtney. And though she applauded Courtney for taking such a firm stand against the Nursing Supervisor that night, Karen, herself, would never have had the nerve.

"Yeah. In a way. I'm supposed to go to some meeting tomorrow with a bunch of big deal administrators. Maggie says it's so they can tell me **what** a naughty girl I was for speaking up."

"Aren't you nervous?" Karen asked.

"You know, it's funny. You would think I'd be **really** nervous. I'm not. I'm too frustrated to be nervous. They're the ones who are going to have some tough questions to answer."

"Like, just what is it that Nursing Supervisors actually do?" Karen laughed.

"Yeah. I guess something to that effect. Only I think I'll try to be a little more tactful with the wording." Courtney was silent for a moment then asked, "Who do you suppose will be there?"

"Alice Erickson, definitely," Karen answered without hesitation. "And maybe even Mr. Proctor. That's how you'll know just how important this meeting is - if he's there, I mean."

"Who's Mr. Proctor?" Courtney had no idea.

"You're kidding. He's only the Chief Executive of the hospital. The guy who signs your paycheck. How can you have worked here for almost a year and not know who he is?"

"I don't pay attention to stuff like that. I'm here to take care of sick patients, not to kow-tow to the politics of the place."

Karen smiled an evil little smile. "Speaking of politics, would you like to know a hot little piece of hospital gossip about old Steve Proctor?"

"Do tell," Courtney said hungrily.

Karen wasted no time in telling her that Alice Erickson, the Administrative Assistant and second-in-command after Steve Proctor, was hot-to-trot for "Stevie." Rumor had it they were having a hot and heavy affair, but that Steve Proctor would never leave his millionaire wife. Alice, however, either didn't believe it or wasn't quite convinced that she didn't still have a chance.

The story was cut short by chimes on the intercom as two patient call lights went on. One of them was Gary Evans' light. "I'll see what Gary wants," Courtney volunteered, "and you get the other one."

Gary was actually beginning to look a little better. He'd been off the ventilator for about a week now and had no further respiratory problems. Of course, he still had the tracheotomy, just in case, but the nurses were now plugging it intermittently to get Gary used to breathing through his nose and mouth again. His face was swollen and puffy both from the surgery and the I.V. steroids he was receiving. His hair was beginning to grow back in uneven patches and there were purple lines drawn on the side of his head to mark the spot at which the radiation treatments were aimed. And in spite of it all, he was smiling when Courtney entered the room.

"Hi," he said, plugging his tracheotomy with a forefinger as Courtney had taught him when they had first removed the plastic tubing from his throat.

"Hi, yourself." Courtney smiled as she walked over to his bed. "What can I do for you?" She automatically covered Gary's other hand with her own. It had become a habit after all the times she had visited him in the I.C.U. She always felt the need to comfort him by holding his hand.

"Can't somebody else come? I didn't mean for you to answer my light." He looked embarrassed.

"What? I'm not good enough to answer your light anymore?" she teased, hoping to make light of whatever it was that was disconcerting him.

"No. It's just that, well, send somebody else in. Please?"

Courtney was curious, but she understood that it was important to let Gary have control over **something**. "O.K., I can take a hint," she smiled and went out to summon Karen.

When Karen finally emerged from Gary's room, Courtney had to know what it was that Gary didn't trust her with. She was more than a little hurt. Karen saw the injured look on Courtney's face and laughed. "Relax," she said. "He just wanted to use the bedpan and was too embarrassed to ask you for it."

Courtney was relieved.

"What I want to know is, how come nobody seems to mind handing **me** a loaded bedpan? Teach me your secret," Karen said, only half joking.

Courtney was anxious to meet Dave across the street at Epstein's Barr when her shift ended. But she couldn't resist stopping in to say goodnight to Gary before leaving. Things like that meant a lot to him and he had been deprived of enough by now.

"Gary?" She said it softly so as not to disturb him if he was sleeping.

"Uh-huh," came the reply in the darkness.

"I'm leaving now. I just wanted to say goodnight."

"You smell good," he said. "Are you going out?"

Courtney had just brushed her hair and put on a touch of perfume. "You should be a detective," she said. "Yes, I'm going out."

"With your boyfriend?"

"Yes, with my boyfriend."

"Where do people go at this time of night?" He was curious.

"The night's still young," Courtney laughed. "But we're just going to be across the street in this little bar where a lot of hospital people hang out." Courtney knew Gary liked to hear details of the outside world. He was such a little prisoner trapped inside this sterile and mechanical hospital world.

"I can't wait 'til I'm old enough to hang out in bars. I'll be in a rock 'n' roll band and hang out all night," he said enthusiastically.

"Will you take requests?" Courtney asked, encouraging the dream.

"You bet! As long as it's **cool** music and not some dorky romantic song," he said with a scowl.

"That gives me seven years to learn some 'cool music,'" she laughed.

"Tommy died, didn't he?" Gary suddenly asked from out of the blue.

Courtney was taken aback by the sudden change of topic and by the fact that Gary knew. It reminded her of when Tommy had said the same thing about his old roommate, Michael McClendon. It was always so hard to deal with this stuff. She always felt so terribly inadequate at these moments. But she knew the biggest mistake she could make would be lying about it.

"Yes, Gary. Tommy died." There was no way to sugar coat it. No pretty way to say it. He had asked the question, so she had to assume he was ready to hear the answer.

"Am I gonna die too?" he asked earnestly. "No one ever tells you stuff like that. But if it's true, I wish someone would tell me."

"We're all going to die. You know that." Courtney was stalling for time. She didn't want to get into this now. She didn't want to think about pain and suffering and young boys agonizing over a terminal illness.

140

She wanted to get away from this horribly sad place. She wanted to be in a place where people were laughing and dancing and **having fun**. But at least she **would** be there in another few minutes. Gary had no such choice.

"Gary," she said as softly as she had ever said anything, "no one really knows anything for sure. No one will come right out and tell you something like that because they have no right to predict the future. And whether we live or die is decided in the future. There are all kinds of predictions that doctors make and then some little squirt like you proves them wrong. It happens more often than you would imagine."

"Yeah. They're called miracles," Gary answered.

"But they happen. And you have to believe that."

"I do. I do believe in miracles. I was just wondering if I **needed** one."

Courtney remembered something. She opened her purse and dug down inside until she came up with a Holy Picture of Saint Jude. "Do you know who this is, Gary?"

"Of course. It says right on the bottom of it: Saint Jude."

"That's right. And do you know what his specialty is?"

"His specialty? Oh, you mean like when you lose something and you pray to Saint Anthony to help you find it? Like finding things is his specialty."

"Right. You must have studied your catechism," she smiled.

"So what is Saint Jude's specialty? I don't think I know that one."

"Well, Saint Jude is my very favorite saint. I call on him all the time. He's the patron saint of things despaired of. In other words, when you're feeling really frightened and hopeless about something, Saint Jude's the

141

one you pray to. He's been known to send a few miracles to people who had totally given up on something. That's why I keep this card with me. I got it when I was a little girl in Catholic school and I used to pray all the time that the school would burn down."

Gary laughed. "Did it?" he asked wide-eyed.

"No. But we moved and I got transferred to a different school. So, in a way, I got my miracle."

"Wow," Gary said, with a noticeable glimmer of hope in his eye.

"I want you to have this picture of Saint Jude to remind you that miracles really do happen. There's a prayer on the back. But Saint Jude's pretty cool. He's not big on formalities. You can just say what you have to say in your own words and he'll hear you."

"Wow! Thanks, Courtney," Gary said as he reached for the card.

"I know it's a little raggedy around the edges, but I've had it since I was a little girl. Sister Mary Michael gave it to me when I won a spelling bee in first grade. Take good care of it for me, O.K.?"

"I promise," Gary said. "Besides, it must be an antique by now," he laughed, the old sparkle back in his eye.

Courtney pretended indignation then laughed and said, "I'm going to go now. I want you to get some sleep. See you tomorrow." And she walked out the door and into the brightness of the corridor thinking, at long last, Sister Mary Michael had served some purpose.

Epstein's Barr was crowded for a Tuesday night. To the casual observer, it might have looked more like a wing of the hospital than a bar. Most of the patrons were wearing either O.R. "greens" or white nurse's uniforms, but hospital veneers were melting like April snow.

Courtney spotted Dave, seated in a booth drinking a beer. There was someone sitting directly across the table from him . . . a man, but Courtney couldn't tell from the back of his head who it was. She smiled

142

as she caught Dave's eye and made her way to the booth where he waited.

As she approached, Dave began to introduce her to the man across the table from him who was drinking an odd brand of beer.

"Courtney Quinn, I'd like you to meet Paul Edwards," Dave said, as he took a swig of beer.

Paul Edwards offered his hand. The hand that had held the motorcycle grips of the Harley so expertly. The hand that had rested on her knee that Saturday. She hadn't seen him since his buddy, Officer Davis, had been transferred to the I.C.U.

"How do you do?" Paul said mischievously to a frustrated Courtney. Obviously, Paul wanted to act, in front of Dave, as though they had never met. It didn't matter to Courtney. She would have been a little uncomfortable either way.

"Paul's a Philadelphia cop," Dave said as he signaled for a waitress.

Courtney tried to look surprised as Paul grinned at her. "So, you must do undercover work," she said. "I never would have taken you for a cop," she added with a taunting edge to her voice.

Paul resisted the fierce urge to say something cute about "undercover" work. Instead he smiled at Courtney and said, "Aren't you the observant one."

Courtney had forgotten just how convincing, not to mention appealing, Paul could be when he was being playful. But she put that thought quickly out of her mind, or at least tried to, as she slid closer to Dave.

Paul only stayed long enough to consume one beer. Then he rose, winked discreetly at Courtney, and bid them goodnight.

"What's the matter, Courtney?" Dave said with concern, "You look awfully tense tonight."

Courtney blushed. "I guess maybe I'm just nervous about that meeting with Administration tomorrow," she sighed, knowing she was only telling a half truth.

"What meeting?" Dave asked.

"Oh, I guess I haven't told you the story. God, so many things happen in one day around here that I forget where we left off."

"I remember," said Dave, delighted. Then, "Oh, you mean where you left off in the story."

"Yes, that's what I mean," said Courtney, ignoring the innuendo. "I'll tell you about it in a minute, but first I want to discuss something else."

"What's that?" Dave asked.

"The note you sent me. The one you wrote on the prescription. I had no idea. I mean, I had hoped, but. . . ."

"You couldn't tell? You couldn't see that I'm in love with you?" Dave looked almost hurt.

"It's a little hard to guess that someone is in love with you when you see him flirting with other women."

"I thought we discussed all that and I apologized."

"We did. You did. And I'm very happy that you love me. It's just that I still don't quite understand the logic."

Dave reached for her hand. He was about to teach her a meaningful lesson. "There is no logic, that's why you don't understand it. It's all about the male ego. That's the reason why we do a lot of the stupid and cruel things we do."

"I still need more of an explanation." She was all ears now.

144

"O.K. Picture this. There's this room with nothing but guys in it. A thousand guys. And this one good-looking woman walks in. You know what every guy in that room is thinking?"

"That he wants to jump her bones," Courtney said disgustedly.

"Wrong. Every single guy in that room is thinking: 'She wants **me**.' That's the way it is. We're born that way."

"Well, that does clear up some of the confusion. I just have one more question."

"Shoot."

"What if I tell you that I love you, too? Would that be enough of an ego boost to keep you from blatantly flirting?"

"Why don't you try it and see?" Dave challenged.

Courtney was silent. She looked down at her glass, then back up at Dave's expectant face. "I love you," she whispered.

"I'll try to be a good boy," he whispered back.

CHAPTER SEVENTEEN

"THE MEETING"

Courtney Quinn recognized Alice Erickson as she was about to cross the street, just a split second after it was too late to pretend she hadn't noticed her. Alice was obviously on her way to the same one o'clock meeting Courtney was going to. After exchanging polite greetings, they stood together on the corner, waiting uncomfortably for the light to turn green.

"I assume you're on your way to the meeting?" Alice inquired politely as they stepped off the curb and made their way through the mid-day crowd.

"Yes, I am. I wasn't sure which building it was in, but it's that gray one there, isn't it?"

Alice nodded as they stepped up onto the sidewalk. The conversation was strained but they were soon distracted by an obstacle in their course. It was an old man, lying on the steam vent, curled around an empty wine bottle. Alice looked at him in disgust. Courtney looked at him with a trace of recognition. It was the Leech Man, the patient who had been so horrified when she and Karen hung leeches from his partly-amputated finger.

Alice began to step over him in as lady-like a manner as she could manage in her narrow, tailored skirt. The old man turned over and looked up to see if he was going to have to fight for this vent, then recognized Courtney.

"Hi, Courtney," he slurred his words as he wiped the drool from his mouth.

Courtney was surprised that he remembered her name. She could not, for the life of her, remember his name. But she certainly remembered his diagnosis and treatment.

"How's the finger?" she asked cheerily.

"Works real good now. I thought you guys was nuts when you hung them leeches offa it, but I guess maybe you do know what you're doing."

The man turned his weather-beaten face back to the street and repositioned himself comfortably around the wine bottle.

Alice stood there completely appalled, both at the man living on the steam vent and at Courtney for knowing him.

"You know him?" she said as soon as she regained her composure.

"Of course. He was a patient on our floor," Courtney said nonchalantly.

"What was that he said about leeches? Did he come in with leeches on him?"

Courtney laughed. "Oh, no. We put them on him. His finger was hanging off when he came in so they took him to the O.R. and replanted it. The latest treatment for promoting good circulation in a case like that is 'Leech Therapy.'"

Courtney noticed the gooseflesh on Alice's arms and the revolted look on her face. Could she actually have been a nurse at one time? Courtney didn't see how. No, Alice definitely belonged in a nice, clean business suit in a nice, clean office, as far away from patients as she could get. Apparently she had found her niche. She was speechless the rest of the way to the meeting.

Steve Proctor, Alice's boss and the Chief Executive of the hospital, was seated in the small Conference Room when Courtney and Alice arrived. Beside him sat Mrs. Cassidy, the Nursing Supervisor, and in the corner chair was a secretary who had obviously been told to take notes during the meeting. Courtney felt her stomach tighten.

147

"Please sit down ladies," Steve Proctor said as he motioned to the two empty chairs across the table from him. Courtney obediently seated herself. Mr. Proctor introduced himself and asked Courtney if she knew everyone in the room. When Courtney looked in the direction of the secretary, Steve Proctor nodded his head and said.

"Oh, that's Mrs. Wilson. My secretary. It's always good to keep notes on anything important enough to demand any time." Courtney wondered if he knew that the hospital grapevine was keeping notes on his hot affair with Alice.

All three administrators were smiling the way a stranger offering candy or a shiny dime would smile at a child. Courtney suddenly felt like she was in a shark tank.

Steve Proctor started the meeting off by producing a copy of the Incident Report Courtney had written the night she had demanded that somebody help her, even if it meant the Supervisor had to get her hands dirty. Apparently no one was pleased by the documentation of a dangerously understaffed ward. It was one thing to complain verbally, she was told. But to put it on an official Incident Report meant that the issue had to be addressed and resolved. The hospital attorneys had strongly advised Mr. Proctor to firmly discourage employees from following this route in the future. Such written documentation could end up in a law suit. This matter had to be nipped in the bud.

"So you see, Miss Quinn," the Chief Executive said with just the right amount of patience in his voice, "it really doesn't do anyone any good when you waste your time filling out Incident Reports for this type of a. . . uh . . . ."

"Incident?" offered Courtney.

"Miss Quinn," he began again. "I understand that you are an excellent nurse. Mrs. Cassidy has had a lot of nice things to say about you."

Courtney interrupted. "I would hope so," she said curtly. "I've worked overtime many a night when she's told me how short staffed they are."

"Yes. And don't think we don't appreciate that," Steve Proctor said smoothly. "But there are going to be times when we just don't <u>have</u> the nurses to staff a ward like yours. It's not that we don't look for them or aren't willing to pay the overtime, we just don't have the manpower."

"Woman-power," Courtney said softly. No one seemed to hear.

Steve Proctor went on as Alice watched him with adoring eyes and Mrs. Cassidy wordlessly nodded her head after every sentence he spoke.

"We advertise in the newspapers and Nursing journals all the time for more nurses. Why, we've even gone so far as to send Nurse Recruiters to the Philippines and to England and Ireland to get nurses. The way I see it, we have left no stone unturned in order to provide you with adequate staffing."

Courtney was unimpressed. The words of Maggie Ruggles were so vivid in her head that she could have sworn Maggie was right there whispering them in her ear. "But why do you suppose you **have** to go overseas to get anyone to work here?" Courtney knew she was treading on thin ice, but Maggie would have been proud of her.

"Well, now, Miss Quinn, I think you know that we are not the only hospital experiencing difficulty in recruiting nurses. Why, there's a nationwide shortage. Even school enrollments are down. It's only going to get worse in the future. I suggest you find a way to cope with it, other than instigating trouble."

"I was documenting a dangerous set of circumstances, not instigating trouble."

Mrs. Cassidy decided to take a crack. "Courtney, I think you are an excellent nurse, so far. You've been here less than a year. That's not a lot of time. Yet you've learned a lot and come a very long way. But part of being a good nurse is knowing how to look at the whole picture,

149

assessing the situation , and establishing priorities."

Steve Proctor was impressed. Cassidy certainly knew how to handle people. Courtney was not as easily impressed.

"Everything was a priority that night, Mrs. Cassidy. I had several patients who belonged in the I.C.U., but they couldn't go because there were no beds. Finally, I had to make a trade with I.C.U. because one of my patients was throwing a Pulmonary Embolus right before my eyes."

"Yes. And you handled it like a pro. You acted like a real veteran that night. I was proud of you."

"You didn't seem so proud when you came up to talk to me."

"If I was short with you, dear, I apologize. I have problems and frustrations, too. But I hope you will always feel free to call me in the future if you have difficulties."

This was unbelievable! Courtney wanted to ask Mrs. Cassidy what she planned to do the next time she was called. Did Proctor and Cassidy honestly think she could be placated with compliments and sweet talk? No wonder Maggie said she could never win an argument with these people.

Steve Proctor clapped his hands together loudly and smiled his best administrative smile. "Well, I'm glad we got that all cleared up," he said cheerily. "Courtney, I think you should accept Mrs. Cassidy's apology and know that you can always call her whenever you have a problem. But let's hope that a situation like this doesn't happen again. I think it was just a case of unfortunate timing more than anything else."

The three administrators smiled at each other and nodded in agreement. Proctor rose from his chair and extended his hand to Courtney.

"I hope we meet under more pleasant circumstances the next time."

He smiled as he shook her hand. And though Alice and Mrs.

150

Cassidy remained seated, Courtney knew this was her cue to leave. She was being excused so that they could discuss her after she left.

Next time I'll take my story to the T.V. stations, she thought as she made her exit.

She heard someone close the door behind her.

"She's a troublemaker," Steve Proctor said to Alice. "Find a way to get rid of her."

CHAPTER EIGHTEEN

"HEROES"

Officer Davis was transferred out of the I.C.U. and back to 6-South. His wounds were healing nicely and the immediate danger of Pulmonary Embolism was past. He had been "Heparinized" in the I.C.U., which meant he'd received intravenous doses of an anticoagulant called Heparin, used to dissolve blood clots and prevent new ones from forming. He was kept on a maintenance dose of the oral medication, Coumadin, another anticoagulant or blood thinner . . . just in case.

There had not been even a hint of retaliation from the street gang that had caused his injuries. But two uniformed police officers were kept stationed outside of his door at all times, and Paul Edwards continued his undercover surveillance . . . just in case.

Courtney was carrying the only set of narcotic keys. One nurse on each shift always counted the number of narcotics both at the beginning and end of her shift and was accountable for all narcotics used during the shift. Each nurse had to document the name of the patient receiving the narcotic, the patient's room number, doctor's name and the time and amount of the drug administered. The keys were kept on a long rope the Charge Nurse usually wore around her neck. Anyone who needed narcotics for their patient had to first get the keys from the Charge Nurse, unlock the cabinet, take what she needed and bring the keys back to the Charge Nurse. Courtney often joked that she spent more time tracking down the keys than she spent giving patients their medication.

As she was measuring l5 ccs of Maalox at her medication cart, she felt the presence of someone beside her. Thinking it was one of the ambulatory patients and not wanting to take her eye off the l5 cc mark, she said absently, "Yes? Can I help you?"

"You sure can," came the voice of Paul Edwards. "You can forget about your doctor boyfriend and go out with me," he said with a grin.

Courtney put the bottle down. "You!" You are a troublemaker. You made me lie right in front of him the other night."

"Nah. That wasn't really a lie. I was just playing a little game. It was fun, don't you think?"

"No. I saw nothing funny about it. It made me uncomfortable." Annoyed, she still couldn't help noticing how adorable his grin was.

"Seriously, Courtney, when can we go out again? I really had a great time that day on the motorcycle."

Courtney looked away. "Really, Paul, I can't."

"Look me in the eye and tell me that. You won't or you can't?"

She looked up at him. "I'm involved with Dave. You know that."

"Yes, I know. I just keep hoping you'll wise up to him. He's not what you think he is. Trust me. I'm a guy, I know these things. He's going to break your heart."

"Well, then, I guess I'll just have to learn the hard way." She smiled, not believing a word of what he'd just said.

"All right. You can't blame me for trying. You know where I am if you change your mind." And he sauntered off toward the kitchen for a little snack.

Visiting hours were over now, but there were still a few stragglers saying long good-byes. Courtney had pushed her medication cart up to an alcove where extra linen was stored. She felt a presence beside her again and was immediately irritated. Paul again. Didn't he know when to quit?

But it wasn't Paul this time. Courtney looked into the face of a bearded, long-haired man she had seen earlier. She had noticed him because he was a little grungy-looking and he hadn't appeared to be visiting anyone. She looked quickly toward the kitchen to signal Paul, but he was nowhere in sight. In fact, for once, the entire corridor was vacant.

The man, looking at her with the dilated pupils of a junkie, had the breath of a camel. He reached out, clasped both ends of the rope that held the narcotic keys and slowly tightened it on her neck. Red lights began flashing and railroad gates came down in her brain with a neon sign that blinked **DANGER! DANGER!** Every horror story she had ever heard of women being attacked by drug-crazed junkies flashed through her mind and every ounce of good sense told her to scream. But her voice wouldn't work.

"Don't be afraid," smiled the junkie, exposing the few rotted teeth left in his mouth. "Just give me the keys and let me get what I want. No one's gonna hurt you. Just give me the keys."

Courtney's back was to the wall and she let herself lean against it. She was going to faint. Her heart was pounding and it was hard to breathe. Oh, she was going to faint all right.

Suddenly, a strong arm grabbed the junkie's comparatively frail arm and twisted it up behind his back, making him whimper and squeal with pain. Paul Edwards' face was grim, his eyes menacing. One of the uniformed officers ran up behind him and handcuffed the addict. It all happened within the blink of an eye.

The uniformed officer stayed with the prisoner and radioed for someone to take him into the police station. Paul looked down at Courtney. She was badly shaken. It was time for a little comic relief. "Now will you go out with me?" he teased.

"Yes," she whispered. Her eyes met his. "Yes."

154

CHAPTER NINETEEN

"JULY FIRST"

Any nurse who works in a hospital long enough, knows about July First. It is a day to be dreaded. The day that, nationwide, all new interns automatically and magically are transformed from medical students to real doctors. Much like turning twenty-one and instantly being considered an adult, becoming an intern has nothing to do with knowledge or experience, and everything to do with the simple fact that now it is "time" to be a doctor.

Nurses and well-educated patients alike dread this day. It is a good idea to plan a day off or postpone your hospital admission on this day. Interns rely heavily on experienced nurses to guide them through managing a patient in crisis. These are the same interns who, later in the year, will forget the nurse's name and the fact that she saved not only their patients' lives but, oftentimes, their medical reputation as well.

It is also a time when interns-about-to-become-residents like to show off for the incoming group of interns. This was the case when Courtney Quinn arrived at the hospital to work her very first July First.

It started off innocently enough. One of the medical interns who, as of today was a resident, was admitting a patient to 6-South. Courtney was looking over the admission orders, which appeared to be pretty routine. Except that all of the bloodwork was ordered to be drawn tonight. Routine bloodwork was usually drawn in the morning, when the Lab had extra personnel working, both to draw the blood and to run the tests. Unless a patient was going for surgery the next morning, bloodwork could usually wait until then to be drawn.

There were several new interns and a few medical students in the Nurses' Station poring over patient charts and trying to look official. Keith Martin, the intern-turned-resident, had just written the orders for bloodwork tonight on this very routine admission. Courtney was trying to organize her tasks for the evening when she came across the orders.

"Keith," she said, looking up from the chart, "why are we getting blood on Mrs. Simpson tonight instead of tomorrow?"

Keith Martin, M.D., looked at her scornfully and said, "Because I ordered it."

"Is she for the O.R. or something?" Courtney asked, giving him the benefit of the doubt and ignoring his rude comment.

"No," was all he said, goading her into a fight.

The new interns and medical students were all ears as they observed this "pro" in action. They were eager to see how a "real" doctor handles a nurse. And Keith Martin was enjoying every minute of it.

"I don't understand," continued Courtney. "It doesn't make any sense to have the only I.V. Nurse in the whole hospital make a trip up here to draw blood that the technicians could draw in the morning. I mean . . . ."

Keith Martin cut her off in his best "Me, doctor; you nurse," voice. "Because I said it should be drawn tonight, that's why," he said loudly enough for all to hear.

"But . . . ." began Courtney, ready to protest the absurdity of such an order. Once again, she was cut off in mid-sentence.

"Look. I'm the doctor. That means I write the orders. Your job is to follow the orders. When you get your degree from medical school, then you can tell me how to write orders."

Courtney knew she was right. And she would not give up, especially since she knew this was all just a big show by Keith Martin to impress the new interns and medical students. Well, she was going to do some impressing of her own.

156

"Look, Keith," she said with fire in her eyes, "if you can give me one good reason why this bloodwork has to be drawn tonight, I have no problem with it. But I get the impression you're just trying to throw your weight around. And I don't like it."

"I don't give a shit whether or not you like it!" Keith came closer to her until she could see clearly the dark circles beneath his eyes from being on-call last night, and she could hear the short staccato breaths of a man who was beginning to hyperventilate. He was obviously stressed out, like an elastic band that was about to snap, instead of stretch. He clenched his fists and towered over her. For a second, Courtney was certain he was going to hit her. She could see him struggling to get hold of himself. She was frightened, but she'd be damned if she would let it show.

She narrowed her eyes and didn't budge from where she stood. "Go ahead. I dare you," she said evenly, never taking her eyes from his frenzied face.

Keith Martin hesitated for a moment, then ripped the chart from Courtney's hands and threw it against the wall. Several pairs of eyes followed the chart as it smashed against the wall, broke apart, and scattered in several different directions on the freshly mopped floor.

"Oh, such a big man," Courtney said, her voice dripping with sarcasm. Then she picked up the phone and dialed the number for Dr. Shaw, the Chairman of the Medical Department and Keith Martin's boss. She spoke to the secretary, never taking her eyes off Keith, and asked that Dr. Shaw please call 6-South regarding the infantile behavior of one of his residents. The new interns and medical students stared mutely and Keith turned and stalked off the ward, his new white lab coat flapping in the breeze.

Lulu, the Housekeeper, appeared out of nowhere and began picking up pieces of the broken chart. Courtney went around the desk and began helping her. Everyone else silently went back to whatever it was they had been doing before the big showdown.

When the phone rang, it wasn't Dr. Shaw returning her call. Instead, it was the Admitting Office informing her that she would be receiving a patient from the Emergency Room. It was a forty-eight-year-old female with a diagnosis of "Multiple Trauma." That diagnosis didn't tell Courtney much. Multiple Trauma meant simply that the patient had more than one injury. It meant anything from a fist fight resulting in multiple bruises to a car accident resulting in broken bones, ruptured organs and a concussion.

The phone rang again, and this time it was Mark Duffy, Orthopedic resident and David Strauss' friend. Apparently Dr. Shaw did not intend to return her call.

"Hey, Courtney." Mark smiled into the phone when he heard her voice. "How ya doin'?"

"Oh, I've had better days," she said truthfully. "What's up?"

"Well, I'm in the Emergency Room with a patient we're gonna send up to you. She's in pretty bad shape. Multiple Trauma from an M.V.A."

"Right. I just got the call from Admitting that we're getting her. What's the story?" Courtney had no idea what a pro she sounded like to the new interns seated at the desk.

"Well, we just finished putting both her legs and one arm in skeletal traction," Mark said matter-of-factly.

Courtney still didn't know that much about Orthopedics, but she knew "skeletal traction" meant that pins were driven through the long bones (in this case, the tibia or shin bone and the humerus, the long bone in the upper arm) and had a good twenty to thirty pounds of weight hanging from them in order to keep the fractured bones in some kind of alignment until they could be surgically stabilized.

"The reason I'm calling is to let you know we're taking her to the O.R. tonight and she needs to be kept N.P.O. Oh, and another thing, Courtney, we put her on some crazy new bed that Administration just ordered. They tell me it's really a big improvement over the old Orthopedic beds for setting up traction. Personally, I don't see any difference. More than likely it's just <u>cheaper</u> than the old beds. Anyway, I'm gonna stick the instructions on how to operate the bed under the foot of the mattress. It's really not complicated but, then, I don't know what you guys have to know about operating this thing."

Courtney smiled. Mark Duffy was always such a pleasure to work with. Why couldn't they all be like him? "O.K., Mark. Thanks for the warning. I'm just surprised that Administration went ahead and ordered a bed without trying it out first or at least asking the nurses for some kind of input."

"C'mon. You know better than that," Mark laughed. "If it's cheaper, it's better, whether or not it's good for the patient."

"Oh, silly me," said Courtney. "I keep forgetting what the priorities are around here."

"That's what they get paid the big bucks for. Making decisions about things they know nothing about." Mark laughed again. "Anyway, when she goes to the O.R., she goes in the bed. Don't let anyone try to transfer her to a gurney with all that traction."

Ten minutes after they hung up the phone, an orderly appeared, pushing a traction-laden bed down the hall to Room 662. Courtney dropped what she was doing and helped the orderly maneuver the cumbersome hodgepodge of patient, traction, I.V., and paperwork toward the door of her room. But the bed wouldn't fit.

Courtney pulled out the directions from under the foot of the mattress where Mark had left them for her. They tried lowering the whole bed, but it was already as low as it could go. They tried a different angle, but the doorway was simply too small to accommodate the bed. Courtney knew that the traction could not be moved because it could easily disturb the alignment of the fractures Mark had just worked on so hard. Patient, nurse and orderly were all exasperated.

Courtney went to the phone and paged the Supervisor, Mrs. Cassidy. She wondered what she could expect this time. She explained the situation and Mrs. Cassidy said only, "Oh, dear."

159

"What should I do?" Courtney asked.

"I'm not sure," replied Mrs. Cassidy. "You're positive it's one of the new beds they just ordered?"

"I'm positive," Courtney answered. "Why? How many of these things did they buy?" she asked, suddenly realizing what an enormous waste of money there had been.

"I think about thirty of them," Mrs. Cassidy said. "But we can't worry about that now. We have to concentrate on getting that patient in a room. Hmmmmm."

"Do you think we could call the O.R. and tell them the problem and see if they can keep her in the holding area 'til her surgery? Then when she's on the table, we can switch back to one of the old beds." Courtney surprised even herself with this very valid plan.

"Yes, Miss Quinn. That's probably the only thing to do. I'll call the O.R. and explain the situation."

Courtney was about to hang up when Ms. Cassidy said "Oh, Miss Quinn, one more thing."

"Yes?"

"I received a call from Dr. Shaw earlier. He said you had some kind of problem up there with one of his residents."

"Yes, I did."

"Well, I wish you had informed me instead of Dr. Shaw. It made me look pretty foolish when he called and I didn't have any idea what he was talking about."

"But I didn't see why I had to get you involved," Courtney answered honestly. "That resident was really out of line. He almost hit me. There were witnesses. I thought I'd handle it myself by documenting it and letting his superiors know what he did."

160

"Well, that was the worst thing you could have done. Dr. Shaw called Steve Proctor about it and I'm afraid he and Alice Erickson would like to have another meeting with you. Tomorrow. At one o'clock again."

Courtney felt she had been tried, found guilty and sentenced without ever having had a chance to tell her side of the story. God only knew what kind of a story Keith Martin had given Dr. Shaw. She had a feeling this meeting was going to be even worse than the first.

She was right.

CHAPTER TWENTY

"THE REAL DAVID STRAUSS"

David Strauss, M.D., had trouble making commitments. It had been a lifelong problem. Of course, on the surface, it all looked very different. Who could say anything like that about a man who had gone through four years of college, four years of medical school, a year of internship and several years of residency? But then, there were always so many choices in the field of medicine, that he was able to switch specialties to his heart's content and still fall under the much-envied and respected title of "Doctor."

It wasn't the same with women. They always found out about each other. They always got jealous. Whoever wrote that song about "Why can't a woman be more like a man?" certainly knew what he was talking about. Not that he didn't like women. In fact, he was fascinated by them. No one enjoyed the company of a woman more than he but, to Dave Strauss, they were all interchangeable. Each one was as delicious as the last one and the next one. They were always so much fun, that is, until they started getting possessive and demanding to know about, and take over, too much of his life.

They all wanted to fall in love. They all wanted to hear the three magic words. Dave had uttered those words a thousand times, for he had found that they were like a master key that opened every door that had been closed to him. He enjoyed a challenge as much as any man, but it was getting too easy now. Sometimes he didn't have to say anything. He could just let the "M.D." after his name do all the talking for him. For some women, that had been all it took. And the women who had been hurt before and so were not as easily impressed, needed only to hear the three magic words, and their hearts were suddenly open and welcoming to him. So he said the three magic words - a lot. And he always got the result he was looking for.

There had been one time, though, when he had meant the words. It had happened a long time ago, back in medical school. Her name was Barbara and she was beautiful. Unlike Dave, she had come from a long line of brilliant and successful doctors, most of them surgeons. Even the textbooks they studied contained quotes from references to her renowned relatives.

Barbara had been driven and brilliant. She could be caring and feminine one minute and aggressive, ambitious and competitive the next. She had kept him completely off balance - something no one before her or anyone after her had ever done. For once in his life, perhaps the only time in his life, he gave himself over to his feelings for a woman. He enjoyed being kept off balance. He even enjoyed arguing with her, because she fought more like a man. There were never any helpless, guilt-producing tears or any irrational, emotional flare-ups. If Barbara was angry, you knew it - because she told you, straight out. There were no sullen looks, no guessing games, no sulking. No, sir, she just let you have it, sometimes even with her fist, and she could always give you a clear, rational reason why she thought you were a jerk. She was usually right. Then all it took was an admission of guilt and sincere apology - just once. After that, the whole thing would blow over and truly be forgotten. She was not like other women, who kept score of how many times you hurt them and who could forgive, but not forget.

She never made excuses for herself. She didn't have to. She never did anything that she didn't plan or research or plot. Everything she did, she did deliberately and with finesse. That's not to say that she couldn't be spontaneous. She once flew to the Bahamas "for lunch," just because she "felt like it." But the one and only time she ever took any real risk, she paid for it. She got pregnant.

When she'd told Dave about it, he was shocked at first. He couldn't imagine that this very responsible woman would have given no thought to protecting herself from getting pregnant. He had just assumed she was using something. She admitted that she usually did, but had just been carried away that one time, on the beach, on the cape, in the moonlight. And, furthermore, she reminded him that his attitude was selfish and chauvinistic - terms which she said defined each other.

After the initial shock wore off, Dave realized he was elated. There

163

was no one in the world with whom he would rather share his gene pool (a rich one, in his opinion) than with Barbara. And though they were both still in medical school, he felt they would work things out. They would marry and find a way (with the help of her very well-to-do family) to both finish med school and start their prospective careers. Life was wonderful.

But Barbara had other plans. And there was no room for marriage and a baby in them. She was lying in bed with her feet propped up on several pillows when he came home to the little apartment they shared on campus. She looked pale and fragile as she lay there, enveloped in white sheets and pillows. She answered his question while it was only in his eyes. Before it reached his mouth. "Yes," she had said. "I had an abortion. I didn't want this baby."

She answered all of his "But what about me?" questions by simply saying it didn't matter whether or not he wanted it, because she absolutely did not want it and that was that. Things were never the same again afterward. The relationship went downhill and the last he'd heard of Barbara was that she was out on the ski slopes in St. Moritz, setting fractured bones and taping sprained ankles.

She had wounded him badly, but he had to admire her style. No long, drawn-out good-byes, no tears, no hope of reconciliation. Cut and dried. The way he liked it, too. But if Barbara had taught him anything, she had taught him that love eventually hurts. And that is why he didn't like commitments. They always got too sticky, too scary, too oppressive. Except, of course, with Barbara. She was the only one. He would have been able to make a commitment to her.

But that was all water under the bridge now. There had been a lot of women parading through his life since then, but no one had even come close to igniting the fire that Barbara had stirred in him. Then he'd met Courtney Quinn, and every now and then he thought he felt the beginnings of that old familiar blaze. But she was so innocent. Still so unspoiled and with the high ideals and altruistic goals of youth. That frightened him. Though there were many lovable things about her, he did not want to be the one to show her what it feels like to have someone walk on your heart, with cleats on. And it was going to happen, sooner

164

or later. Courtney was the kind of girl who wanted monogamy and commitment and Dave just didn't think he was capable of it.

He continued to see other women on the side. It was easy to do with her working the 3 to 11 shift most days. This way he could have a loving relationship with Courtney and keep his freedom, too. And he **did** love her. Those had not just been meaningless words as they were with the others. But he simply had lost the part of himself that was capable of commitment. He had lost it a long, long time ago. It was something like when a wild animal gets its foot caught in a trap. Oftentimes it will chew the ensnared foot off, just to have its freedom - even though now it has to survive in the wilderness with a handicap. Its freedom is that precious.

Dave wanted to tell Courtney all of this. He wanted to explain it. But he was afraid he wouldn't do a very good job and she would be confused and hurt. It was much easier to just sabotage this relationship as he had all the others. It made him look better.

And that is why, when Courtney Quinn was crossing the street to go to her second meeting with Steve Proctor, Alice Erickson and Mrs. Cassidy, she ran into Dave . . . with a girl on his arm.

Much to her credit, she did not lash out or demand embarrassing explanations right there in the street. It was worse. The hurt in her eyes was evident. He could almost hear her heart breaking. The doctor in him wanted to fix it and make it all better. The wild animal in him wanted to chew off the part of his heart that belonged to Courtney and head for the hills, taking his chances with the hunters.

CHAPTER TWENTY-ONE

"THE DECISION"

"Well, I see we meet again, Miss Quinn," Steve Proctor said, extending his hand as Courtney entered the Conference Room. Alice Erickson and Mrs. Cassidy nodded to her and she took a seat. It was like a re-run of the previous meeting. It was the same Conference Room with the same secretary sitting in the same corner taking notes. Everyone was seated in the same chairs as before, wearing the same administrative smiles.

"Well, I'll get right to the point, Miss Quinn. You're here because Dr. Shaw tells us that you called his office in regard to an incident involving one of the medical residents. A Keith Martin, I believe," Proctor said, looking down at some notes in front of him.

"That's right," Courtney nodded. She had the strangest feeling this conversation was being tape recorded.

"Would you like to tell us what happened?" He smiled like a wolf in sheep's clothing.

There was nothing she would have liked less. But she knew he didn't mean that she had any choice. She told the whole miserable story, starting with the way she was trying to save the only I.V. Nurse in the whole hospital from having to make an unnecessary trip, and ending with Keith Martin clenching his fists and throwing the chart. She got the distinct impression they thought she was exaggerating.

"Alice," Proctor said, "would you like to start by telling Miss Quinn where she went wrong?"

Alice was only too happy to do anything that her Steve asked of her, and do it well. She was also only too happy to have found Courtney at fault again, since Steve's underlying goal was to find a reason to get rid of her before she caused any more problems.

"Certainly, Steve." Alice smiled with something just short of a wink in her eye. "It seems to me you made three mistakes," she said, turning to Courtney. "The first and most serious one was not only taking matters into your own hands, but also not informing your Supervisor of your actions. I'm sure Mrs. Cassidy felt more than a little foolish when Dr. Shaw called her with this story and she knew nothing about it."

Courtney still hadn't learned that these meetings were a lot like going to court: The less you say, the better. "But if Dr. Shaw had called me instead of Mrs. Cassidy, the whole thing could have been settled right there and then," she blurted out. "It seems to me that if everyone around here communicated more directly, we wouldn't waste so much time in meetings."

"Dr. Shaw is a busy man, Miss Quinn," Proctor interjected. "He doesn't have time to go calling every nurse who is put out by one of his residents writing more orders that perhaps he should."

"And I'm not busy, too? Or is it that because I'm just a nurse, I'm not important enough to warrant a phone call from Dr. Shaw?" Courtney caught the admonishing look that Mrs. Cassidy shot at her, warning her that, once again, she was treading on thin ice.

"There is such a thing called 'chain of command,' Miss Quinn. I won't go into it right now, but I suggest you make yourself familiar with the concept," Steve Proctor said a little too patiently. Courtney could smell trouble in the air.

Alice went on only after she was certain Steve was through. "The second mistake you made was embarrassing Dr. Martin in front of his colleagues who were present at the time."

"He embarrassed himself!" Courtney shot back before she felt the kick under the table from Mrs. Cassidy and before she could stop herself.

"That may very well be," Alice replied smoothly, "but there was no

167

need for you to make a production out of calling Dr. Shaw."

"He threw a chart!"

Everyone ignored her.

"The third mistake you made was in refusing to carry out the order after you had clarified it with the resident who wanted that blood drawn. That's not to say you can never question a doctor's order. I'm saying simply that, once you question it and the doctor clarifies it, there is no reason to carry on any further."

"Very well done," Steve Proctor smiled at Alice.

"But the order was unnecessary," Courtney continued. "And he only realized it after I pointed it out to him. By then he was too proud to change it and put on this macho show of slinging the chart into the wall. He had an audience and he was performing for them. It was very insulting to me."

"Perhaps you're just a little too sensitive, Miss Quinn," Steve suggested.

Courtney knew she was defeated. She thought of Maggie Ruggles with new regard. How did that saying go? "Walk a mile in my shoes." Well, Courtney had only taken her first few tottering steps compared to the twenty-two-year career of Maggie Ruggles, and she didn't much care for it. No wonder Maggie was so cynical, so burned out.

"A copy of the transcript of this meeting and our first meeting will be placed in your permanent file, Miss Quinn. Any further problems will also be documented and kept track of," Steve Proctor was saying as Alice and Mrs. Cassidy paid strict attention and nodded their heads at all the right points.

"Are there any questions before we adjourn this meeting?" Steve asked, looking directly at Courtney and not expecting her to have any questions.

"Yes, I have a question," Courtney heard herself say.

Steve only nodded permission to speak. He was getting tired off this young nurse's inability to drop the subject and to know when to shut up.

"What about those thirty new Orthopedic beds you just bought? Do you know they don't fit through the doorways of the patients' rooms?"

"What?" said Steve, turning to Alice who did her best to flutter her eyelashes as she stalled for time. "Are those the new beds you had me approve by signature on the request?"

"Weeeeell, yes," Alice said slowly. "I, uh, I thought I told you about that, Steve."

"This is the first I've heard about it. How many of them did we buy, twenty?"

"Thirty," Alice muttered.

"Of all the stupid mis . . . ." Steve caught himself before he went on berating Alice for her stupidity. This was getting embarrassing. Especially in front off this Quinn girl. He had just reprimanded her for not informing her superiors of what was going on, and here was his assistant making the same kind of mistake right in front of her. Not to mention the stupidity of a mistake like buying all new beds without checking to make sure they fit through the doorways first. Steve did not like losing face like this, especially in front off such a troublesome employee.

"You may be excused, Miss Quinn," Proctor said with false calm.

Courtney rose and wordlessly left the room, remembering to close the door behind her so they could talk about her when she was out of earshot. She had brought a uniform with her, since she had to be at work at three o'clock. She decided to go across the street to the hospital and change her clothes in the locker room. If it was still early enough, maybe she'd sit and visit with Gary Evans for a while. Right now, he was the only person who could possibly have any idea how miserable she felt.

169

She thought about Dave as she stepped over the Leech Man and crossed the street. Who was that girl who had been hanging on his arm when she saw him earlier? She hadn't looked familiar. At least, she wasn't from the hospital. Courtney had to put the whole thing our of her mind until after the meeting. She had promised herself that she would cry later, after Proctor and the others were through with her. But now she was too numb to cry.

She walked along the sunny street. The city was sweltering in the early July heat. There was not even the slightest hint of a breeze or a break in the temperature. The air conditioned atmosphere of the main lobby was a welcome relief as she entered the hospital. But nothing could relieve the heaviness in her heart. Why did Dave have to be such a flirt? Now she wished with all her heart that Paul Edwards would ask her out again, but that was like whistling in the dark. Besides, Officer Davis had been discharged some time ago and there was no reason for Paul to stop up on the floor anymore. If only she hadn't changed her mind after the night he rescued her from the junkie who tried to take the narcotic keys from her. She had been so grateful to him that night, that she'd agreed to go out with him. But then, after regaining her composure and thinking about Dave, she had changed her mind again and had played the whole thing off as a joke. Paul was very gracious about it and had never asked her out again.

The elevators were taking too long, as usual, and there was an enormous crowd of people waiting for them. Courtney didn't feel like being squashed in an elevator with a bunch of strangers in one hundred degree heat. She decided to take the stairs instead. Things couldn't get much worse, she was thinking as she entered the stairwell and began trudging slowly up the deserted stairs. She liked taking the stairs, it gave her time to think. But the more she thought, the worse she felt. She wondered why she couldn't see Dave for the ladies' man he was. He would never change. He didn't want to. Either she had to accept him as he was or get out now, before she got hurt any more.

She decided to get out, but it hurt anyway. She thought about her career. Did she really want to do this for the rest of her life? Would she even be <u>able</u> to do this for the rest of her life? And not just for physical reasons. How many more meetings with the Steve Proctors and Alice

Ericksons of the world could she take? How many more Tommys and Michaels could she watch die? How many rude and scornful interns could her self-esteem take, before buckling from the weight of it. She stopped climbing the stairs. It was getting hard to breathe. She took a big gulp of air and spewed it out in a giant sob. A waterfall of tears followed. She sat in a heap on the bottom step of the landing and allowed herself the luxury of a much needed cry.

"I thought I heard water drippin' on my fresh cleaned floor," came a voice that echoed through the stairwell. "Didn't think it was tears though."

Lulu waddled over and settled her bulky frame on the stairs beside Courtney. "You wanna talk about it, darlin'?" she asked in the soothing way that only someone who is a mother can ask.

"I don't even know where to start," Courtney sobbed. "I guess it's a little bit of everything."

"C'mon now, tell me all about it," Lulu soothed. "Who's hurtin' you? Is it Dr. Dave?"

"Well, yes, in a way."

"In a big way, if you ask me," Lulu corrected.

Courtney looked up with tear-filled eyes. "I love him, Lulu, but he'll never settle down. He can't seem to be happy with just one woman. Either that or I'm just not woman enough for him."

"Oh, hush now," Lulu said in a scolding tone. "You are plenty of woman. And any man who can't see that's gotta be deaf, dumb and blind. Now don't get me wrong, honey. I likes Dr. Dave. But I got a big advantage. I don't want to marry him."

"That is a big advantage," Courtney almost laughed, but she was still crying too hard. "I'd like him a lot better if I didn't love him so much."

"You got that right, sugar." Lulu laughed hard enough for both of

171

them. "Dr. Dave ain't never gonna settle down. He enjoys women too much. A man like that will bring you nothin' but heartache."

"He already has," Courtney sobbed.

"Now you take a man like that police officer that used to be hangin' around you. What was his name? Edwards or something?"

"Yes, Paul Edwards." What a coincidence that Lulu would mention him. She was a lot more observant than she appeared. Courtney's tears subsided.

"Yeah, that's it. Officer Edwards. He was a fine looking man. And he was crazy about you, honey," Lulu said with a faraway look in her eye.

"Yeah, but I pretty much burned my bridges with him. I turned him down every time he asked me for a date. Well, except for once. I really had a good time, too," Courtney said a bit dreamily. "I wonder why I never gave him more of a chance?"

"'Cause Dr. Dave was turnin' your head with all his charm," Lulu mused. "Now a man like Officer Edwards, he's the marryin' kind. He won't do you wrong. Trust me, I know about these things."

"Well, it's too late now. I'll probably never run into him again anyway." Courtney sniffled and Lulu pulled a Kleenex from her pocket and handed it to her.

"And then there's this job," Courtney continued after blowing her nose. "It's just too much. It seems like I'm always getting in trouble just because I want to do too good a job. I can't take this place anymore. I guess I just don't have what it takes to be a good nurse."

Lulu looked at Courtney for a long moment. "Shoot, girl, you lost your mind or somethin' in this heat? You're plenty good. And you're strong too. Fact is, I think you got a lotta spunk, 'specially for a white girl."

Courtney was beginning to feel better.

Lulu went on. "I ain't never seen no nurse stand up to those doctors like you do, 'cept for Maggie Ruggles an she don't count 'cause she's got quite a head start on you. And you know what else?"

"What?" Courtney sniffled again.

"I ain't never seen nobody else have the gumption to write an Incident Report accusin' Administration of negligence. Oooweee. Girl, I was sure proud of you that day. Now you gonna let a silly little meeting with a bunch of good fo' nothin' administrators do you in? Shoot, girl. It ain't worth one of your tears."

"But you know what else it is, Lulu?" Courtney said pensively. She didn't wait for an answer. "I'm just so tired. I'm tired of being so responsible, of being everybody's mother. I feel so empty and 'gived out.'"

They both sat silently for a moment and Courtney's sniffles echoed in the stairwell.

"I don't want to be a nurse anymore." She said it softly, eyes staring straight ahead in what they used to call "the thousand yard stare."

Lulu mulled it over. She could certainly see why Courtney felt this way. "I can't say as I blame you, sugar. I wouldn't want your job. Shoot, even _my_ job is better'n yours," she grinned.

Courtney giggled. "You might have something there, Lulu. At least I'd have more holidays and weekends off than I do now." She was actually smiling. "And no rotating shifts," she added.

"Yeah," Lulu's layers of belly began to heave with laughter. "Just think. You could transfer to Housekeeping. I'd pay to see the look on old Steve Proctor's face when he got that news." Both women filled the stairwell with echoes of heartfelt laughter. Tears of hilarity rolled down both faces.

173

Lulu was gasping for air between waves of laughter. Courtney then turned to her, completely deadpan. "Lulu, I'm going to do it," she said.

"Oh, child. Please don't make me laugh no mo'. My stomach hurts, girl."

"What kind of salary would I make?" Courtney continued. "Never mind. I have some money put away. I could live off of that while I'm proving a point." Courtney's face was intense and the old enthusiasm and spunk were back.

"Girl, you serious, ain't you?" Lulu marveled.

"Damn right I'm serious. Don't try to talk me out of it either. It's perfect. Do you know how embarrassing it will be to them when people find out that a nurse is transferring to Housekeeping because of the conditions of her job? It's the absolute perfect way to prove a point. My mind is made up. Nothing will change it."

Lulu studied the determined look on Courtney's face and murmured to herself.

"I wouldn't even try."

CHAPTER TWENTY-TWO

"THE METAMORPHOSIS"

"What the hell is this?" Steve Proctor exploded into the phone. "I'm looking at a request on my desk from Courtney Quinn, R.N. to transfer to the Housekeeping Department. What the hell is going on around here and why can't you keep these nurses in line!?"

"I was going to discuss it with you, Steve," Alice Erickson said in her best, administratively calm voice. "I didn't realize that Personnel would send the request directly to you."

"You bet your ass they did. They're the only ones around here with any sense."

"Steve, I didn't know how to stop her. I discussed it with Mike in Personnel and he says that there is no way to stop her. Intra-departmental transfers are based on past job performances and seniority. Courtney has a flawless record as far as her work is concerned and she's been with the hospital for almost a year now. Besides, there's not exactly a lot of competition to transfer to the Housekeeping Department. Mike says we have to give it to her."

"She's obviously trying to embarrass us somehow. She's a real troublemaker. I thought I told you to find a way to get rid of her before something like this happened."

"It's not that easy, Steve."

"Bullshit. She's human isn't she?"

"Yes, but she's no dummy. First of all, her clinical abilities and performance as a nurse are above reproach. It would be very tough to nail her on anything like that. And secondly, she tends to be a bit of a rebel. She won't hesitate to make a major issue out of anything we do to her. She has to be handled very carefully."

There was silence on the other end of the phone. Alice wasn't sure if this was a good sign or a bad sign. She tempered her voice with just the right mixture of competence and seduction.

"Steve?" she purred into the phone.

"I'm thinking," he snapped. "O.K., here's what we'll do with Miss Smarty-pants. We'll give her exactly what she asked for. She wants to work in Housekeeping? Then that's exactly what she'll do. My money says she won't last a week."

"I'm sure you're right, Steve. You always are." Honey was dripping from her voice. Alice Erickson wanted Steve Proctor <u>BAD</u>.

"Put her transfer through right away. And who's the head of the Housekeeping Department? Is it Bill Stevens?"

"Yes, that's right."

"Well, give him a call and explain the situation. Tell him to lean extra hard on her."

"Of course. I'll do it right away," Alice answered.

"And make sure she gets the most distasteful assignment we have. I want this to be a truly humbling experience for her."

"Consider it done," Alice said obediently.

"And, Alice, one more thing."

"Yes?"

"I have some free time today between one and two. How about you?"

"What a coincidence. So do I."

······

Courtney decided to write a letter to Alice Erickson explaining her bizarre request for a transfer to Housekeeping. Not that she thought she owed anyone an explanation, but she was more interested in having the letter placed in her permanent file, which is where she knew it would end up.

She still had some time before going to work. She would write it now and drop it off on her way to 6-South. She was something of a heroine, lately, ever since her announcement that she was transferring to Housekeeping. After they stopped laughing, most nurses thought it was a great idea and that more people should do it. But, of course, they would wait and see how Courtney made out first.

Then again, some of the reactions were mixed. Maggie Ruggles treated Courtney with new respect. Karen Beal said she thought Courtney should reconsider the possible consequences. And Dave said she shouldn't lower herself to this, that she was a professional and she should find a more "professional" way to resolve the conflict.

She had called him the day after she had seen him on the street with another woman. She tried to tell him what that did to her. That she was beginning to feel like just one of his harem and she didn't like it. She couldn't live that way. Dave admitted that he had more than one "other woman" and that he didn't plan to change that. The lifestyle suited him just fine. He was sorry he had hurt Courtney, but he hoped they could remain friends. Courtney had wanted a more emotional conversation with him. The things he said and the way he had said them sounded well practiced, as if he had said the same things a thousand times. And he had.

In an effort to prove that he wanted to remain on friendly terms, Dave had asked Courtney about her meeting the other day. She told him everything that had happened and about her plan to embarrass them by transferring to Housekeeping. She explained that she wanted to

177

make an example of the unfair stresses placed on the nurses (like short staffing and little or no administrative support) by transferring to one of the most distasteful jobs available and calling it an improvement.

She really didn't care that Dave disapproved of this move. She was through with trying to win his approval. On the surface, she would remain friendly with him if that's the way he wanted it but, deep in her heart, things would never be the same. How could they be? She was ready now and strong enough now to end this painful relationship.

What had happened to her, she wondered. Although it hurt to end this relationship, it hadn't hurt nearly as badly as she had thought it would. And she was ending her career to, at least for a time, and that didn't hurt much either. Was she just becoming numb? Or was she finally growing up and getting far enough away from the attitude produced by her three mortal sins; Being female, Catholic and a nurse? She was doing some growing up and learning some hard lessons, she decided. And she was proud of herself. She knew she deserved more than a boyfriend who couldn't let go of the other women in his life, and a profession that took advantage of her and expected her to keep quiet about it and be a good little girl. Her self-respect and personal moral codes were blossoming and she liked it, no matter what it might cost.

She sat back and thought about the two big steps she was taking. She realized they were long overdue. Most importantly, she would stop giving for awhile. She had given far too much of herself and everyone kept asking for more. But she had never stopped and let anyone put something back. Courtney would never let that happen again. People would always keep asking, no doubt. Asking for just one more small favor, one more minute of her time, one more dagger in her heart, one more bedpan, one more pain pill, one more anything, just to keep her giving. But that would all change now.

She picked up her pen to start the letter to Alice. She felt better already.

CHAPTER TWENTY-THREE

"MAKING MIRACLES"

Courtney came to work on Friday in a lighthearted mood. This was to be her last official day as a nurse. Her request for a transfer to Housekeeping had gone through without a hitch. She was to begin Monday. So after finishing her shift tonight, she would have the whole weekend off to switch gears, so to speak.

She was surprised, and maybe a little disappointed, that it all had gone so smoothly. She had expected that such a rash reaction on her part might have made the administrators think twice and maybe come up with some kind of plan or a compromise to get better staffing. It was for the sake of the patients as well as the nurses that Courtney was fighting. She had suggested they take all the money they used for a full-time Nurse Recruiter's salary, and weekly newspaper and television and radio ads, not to mention the cost of trips to the Philippines, etc., and put that money toward paying nurses higher salaries. It was Courtney's belief that there were plenty of nurses out there. They just didn't want to work in hospitals anymore. Where were all the women of Maggie Ruggles' generation? The ones who'd had no choice but to be teachers or nurses? They were out there, to be sure. The hospitals just needed to make working in them more attractive.

Courtney had truly expected that Alice Erickson or Steve Proctor, or both of them, would try to prevent the embarrassment of having a nurse transfer to Housekeeping because the working conditions were better. But they hadn't tried to stop her. In fact, the secretary over in Personnel had called yesterday to tell her she could start on Monday and that she should report to the Housekeeping office on the ground floor of the main building for her assignment.

Courtney certainly didn't see working in Housekeeping as her new career. She saw it simply as a vehicle to get her message across. And she was going to do everything she could to publicize the fact that the reason there was such a severe shortage of nurses was because of the poor working conditions and lack of respect and support. Generation after generation of nurses had just stood quietly by and endured the sometimes unbearable conditions and stresses of their jobs. Nurses had never necessarily been known as fighters. They were givers, and quiet givers at that.

She didn't want to be like Maggie Ruggles and the other more experienced ones who were just plain bitter, but who did nothing but complain. Courtney would always be a nurse, whether she was employed as one or not. But she felt a need to speak up for nurses now, to put on a dramatic show to draw attention to their plight - because no one ever had. Clearly, it was time to stop complaining and **do** something about the situation. After that, who knew? She would play it by ear. But, in all honesty, she had to admit she was a bit apprehensive.

But she wasn't going to think about that now. She didn't have time to. For one more night, she was still a nurse and the chaos of the ward took top priority in her thoughts.

She learned, during Change of Shift Report, that three new patients from a motor vehicle accident were being admitted to 6-South. They each had a diagnosis of multiple trauma and each had to be watched closely. Then there was the news of another fight among the street gangs, and several of them were in the Emergency Room with gunshot and stab wounds. The Admitting Office was going crazy trying to find beds for all of them. Clearly, there would be beds set up in the Conference Room tonight and Courtney was informed that 6-South would be accommodating at least one of the patients from the street gangs.

She hung up the phone and looked up just as a group of perplexed doctors were emerging from Gary Evans' room. They meandered past the Nurses' Station lighting pipes and wiping eyeglasses and philosophizing.

"I don't understand it. I've never seen anything like this before. Yet how can three C.A.T. Scans be wrong?" mused one of the doctors.

180

"He's young," offered another. "I've seen odd things happen before, when it comes to kids. Kids can fool you. They're very resilient. But sooner or later, a tumor like this is gonna kill you. I don't care what you say."

"I agree, Pete," said a third doctor. "I think perhaps he's just in some kind of remission. A tumor like that doesn't just go away."

"Unless we mis-diagnosed him in the first place," the first doctor offered. "But I don't see how."

Courtney was stunned. Were they talking about Gary? Were they saying that his tumor was shrinking? That he was getting better? Had Gary received his miracle? And if he had, no wonder these doctors were so baffled. They couldn't possibly understand. They were only scientists. Naturally, they would be far more comfortable calling it a mis-diagnosis rather than a miracle.

Courtney knew that Gary slept with the holy card of Saint Jude ever since the night she had given it to him. Gary had said that he had no doubt that he "qualified" for a miracle from Saint Jude. And with his child's faith, he had believed wholeheartedly that Saint Jude wouldn't let him down. There had been subtle but noticeable changes in Gary lately. Some of the changes, like the pink glow that was creeping back into his cheeks and the easy way he laughed these days, were hard to document or measure, but they were there nonetheless. The nurses had been the first to notice these changes, but the doctors tended to ignore such intangible signs of progress. They didn't believe anything unless it could be measured in kilograms or centimeters. Well, now they had a shrinking brain tumor - that they could measure.

The team of doctors shuffled off the ward, still murmuring ominous predictions, still unwilling to trust Gary's apparent good fortune. Gary's sister and mother then emerged from the room, wearing smiles that lit up even these drab, old corridors.

"Courtney," hailed Gary's sister, Kathryn. "Did you hear the news?"

"I think I have an idea, but tell me anyway," smiled Courtney.

"Gary's getting much better." Her face was glowing. "The tumor is shrinking. It's almost completely gone."

Gary's mother then came over and hugged Courtney. "I'm so happy," she sobbed. "He's getting better. The tumor is shrinking. I'm so grateful to you, Courtney."

"Grateful to me?" Courtney was confused. "I didn't have anything to do with it."

"It doesn't matter," his mother wept. "You helped him in a very special way. He's crazy about you, you know . . . and so are we."

Courtney thought her heart might burst with elation for these people. This was a whole lot better than the day Mrs. Evans had come to her with tears in her eyes because she had just seen the diagnosis on Gary's chart. Oh, this was so much better. This was the kind of reward that must be what keeps people in Nursing, despite all the problems and hard work and let-downs. This was the kind of experience that could keep you going through the hard times. Suddenly she was overwhelmed with sadness that she would be leaving Nursing after tonight, at least for awhile. She wanted to stay now. She wanted to wallow in this moment forever. But even in the midst of this euphoria, she knew the moment couldn't last forever, and knew, as well, the bad times and short staffing and overwhelming responsibilities would wash over her like a tidal wave, again and again.

Still, true to her modus operandi, Courtney Quinn could not rest until she knew she had done her part to improve the situation. She had no choice. She didn't apologize for it either. It was what she was all about.

· · · · ·

The double doors to 6-South burst open and a gurney carrying a patient from the gang war was pushed through by a group of people. An

182

orderly pushed the stretcher from behind and an intern walked along beside with his finger on the patient's pulse and a concerned frown on his face. A uniformed police officer walked along the other side of the stretcher, and slightly behind the whole entourage walked Paul Edwards.

"What room?" inquired the orderly as they approached the Nurses' Station.

"I'm gonna need some sterile four-by-fours and some silk sutures!" demanded the intern as they passed the desk.

"Good evening," Paul Edwards murmured with his familiar, calm, stunning smile as he unobtrusively followed in their wake.

Courtney was dumbfounded. First of all, no one had called from the Emergency Room to say they were sending the patient up. Secondly, she didn't have the extra bed set up yet in the Conference Room. And thirdly, Paul Edwards was back!

She quickly got herself organized and made the appropriate phone calls to Housekeeping for a bed, and to the Emergency Room for some kind of a report on the patient. Surely, this night was going to fly. And fly, it did.

Paul Edwards was working under cover again. Apparently, the patient they were guarding this time was a member of the street gangs, but he was also a police informant and it was in their best interest to protect him. Paul had a ringside seat to the pandemonium of the ward that was now routine to Courtney. He was like a fly on the wall as he watched her handle phone calls and talk to irate visitors and administer medications and keep the various interns up to date on what was happening with their patients. She had a certain air of confidence about her now that she hadn't had when he first met her. It made her even more appealing. Paul couldn't help but wonder if she was still involved with Dave Strauss. He didn't want to get his hopes up.

Courtney dashed from one patient to the next and, in between, she answered the ringing telephone that Wanda the Ward Clerk was too busy or distracted to answer. She finally found a free couple of minutes to spend with Gary. She didn't have enough time to eat a meal, but the few free minutes she did have would be spent with him. She had looked forward to it for most of the evening.

"Hi, brat," she smiled at him from the doorway.

Gary was sitting up in bed eating what was left of a pepperoni pizza. No longer did he have the intravenous fluids running into his veins. His appetite had returned to normal and the I.V. had been discontinued. The tube that had been draining his bladder since the night before surgery had been removed, too, and Gary had quickly regained bladder control. The cannula from his tracheotomy had been removed and a small two-by-two dressing covered the site where it had been. Soon the only proof of it would be a tiny scar between his two collar bones. And, best of all, his hair was growing back, thicker and shinier than ever.

"Hi, Courtney." His words were muffled by a mouthful of pizza.

"I heard you've had some pretty good news lately," Courtney mentioned with deliberate nonchalance.

Gary's eyes lit up. "Yeah! That Saint Jude thing really works."

"Saint Jude **THING**?" Courtney laughed.

"Well, you know what I mean. Anyway, ever since you gave me the holy card, I kept it inside my pillow case and, every time I get scared of dying, I take it out and say the prayer that's written on the back. I swear it works, Courtney. The doctors did three C.A.T. Scans before they believed it for themselves that my tumor is almost completely gone."

"I believe it," Courtney said softly. "And what does it matter whether it was a miracle from Saint Jude or maybe the radiation treatments kicking in. The point is that it's shrinking and that you're feeling better."

But Gary was adamant. "The point is that I got a miracle. I figured that if Saint Jude is the patron saint of the hopeless, then he must be **my** patron saint. I knew he'd come through for me. I just knew it."

184

Courtney laughed. She loved watching his innocent and believing face. She wished she still had faith like that. The doctors had told Gary and his family that this surge of good health might only be temporary, but Gary was certain it was permanent. And Courtney would put her money on Gary's opinion any day. "I'm glad you're feeling better. I'd heard about it but I had to see for myself. I have to get back out to work now. But I'm so glad to see you feeling better."

"I'm not just feeling better, I **am** better," he insisted.

"Oh, no. Does this mean you'll be getting in my way now?" Courtney teased.

"Yup," he said smugly and Courtney headed for the door. But before she reached it, Gary stopped the playfulness and called her name.

She stopped in the doorway and turned around. "Yes?"

"Thanks a lot," Gary's eyes were downcast shyly. Then, raising them up to meet hers, he added, "for everything."

She was quiet for a moment. "Thank Saint Jude." She was smiling as she slipped back out into the corridor.

Paul Edwards was standing at the desk when Courtney reached the Nurses' Station. "Was that the kid that was here the last time? The one with the brain tumor?" he asked.

"Yup. Same kid," Courtney said proudly.

"Wow, what did you do to him? He looks great."

"Just told him to have a little faith in miracles, that's all. He did the rest. Well," she corrected herself, "he and Saint Jude did the rest."

"That's pretty impressive coming from a person who seems to have very little faith herself," Paul commented, once again seeing right through her.

Courtney was uncomfortable. She didn't know what to say. She didn't have to. Paul picked up the conversation again. "You've really done some changing since the last time I saw you," he observed.

"I have?" Courtney was surprised.

"I'll say," he chuckled. "You used to look so timid and unsure of yourself. Now you run around here like a pro, ordering people around and . . . ."

"I don't order people around," she said defensively, but with a blushing smile.

"Compared to before you do. What's come over you anyway? I mean, I like the changes, I'm just surprised, that's all."

"Well, take a good look because tonight's my last night as a nurse," she said with a hint of sadness in her voice. She told Paul the whole story of her meetings with Alice and Steve and Mrs. Cassidy and how she'd decided to transfer to Housekeeping, just to prove a point. Paul roared with laughter when she told him she was really going to start her new job on Monday.

"I think you're great, Courtney Quinn," he said with sincere admiration. "Not too many people will still fight for a cause like that. You are truly refreshing."

"Thank you," she said simply. It felt good to have someone else reinforce what she had decided to do.

"One question, though," he added.

"Yes?"

"What does your hot-shot, doctor boyfriend think of all this?"

Courtney winced almost imperceptibly. "He doesn't think it's a very good idea," she said quietly. "He says I shouldn't degrade myself this way."

"You're degrading yourself more by not putting up a fight," Paul said kindly.

"That's what I said!" Courtney was enthused again.

"Have you thought about getting some publicity for this little stunt?"

"Well, I was hoping it would be embarrassing enough just for other nurses to see what I'm doing and maybe jump on the band wagon."

Paul laughed. "No, no. What you need is some real publicity. You know, newspapers, television cameras. That's how to put the pressure on them. The administrators aren't going to care if you rot in the Housekeeping Department, just as long as you rot quietly. What they **don't** want is for the paying public to know how shabbily they treat their nurses."

What he was saying made perfect sense to Courtney. He was right. The hospital couldn't afford any bad publicity. All she had to do now was figure out a way to get the media interested enough to give her the exposure she needed. "But, how. . . .?"

"That's simple," Paul said. "I have lots of friends. Just leave it to me."

He was laughing and Courtney was wishing he would ask her out again. She was trying to think of a subtle way to mention that she wasn't seeing Dave anymore.

And then it occurred to her. Why did she have to be subtle? Isn't that what this whole thing was about? About asking for what you want and going after it? The time had come.

"Paul, I, uh . . . I'm not seeing Dave Strauss anymore."

Paul raised his eyebrows, but said nothing. He wanted to watch the changes in Courtney Quinn.

"I know that when you asked me for a date, I kept turning you down." She was struggling with this, but she was going to do it. Paul waited patiently.

"I guess what I'm saying so eloquently here," she smiled at herself, "is, if the offer still stands, I'd like that a lot."

"The offer never stopped standing," he grinned.

CHAPTER TWENTY-FOUR

"FAME"

Flashbulbs popped and microphones were shoved in her face as Courtney Quinn, R.N., B.S.N., arrived at the hospital for her first day as a member of the Housekeeping Department. She felt more than a little uncomfortable as she made her way up the front steps wearing the unfamiliar turquoise uniform. Paul had said he had friends in the news media who would be glad to do a story on her one-woman-crusade against hospital Administration, but Courtney never guessed it would be anything like this. She felt simultaneously exhilarated and embarrassed.

Directly in front of her, posed on the hospital stairs, stood a picture-perfect T.V. newswoman looking directly into the camera before her and discussing the nation's critical shortage of nurses. The cameraman made sure he got a shot of Courtney in her Housekeeper's uniform in the background, as the news reporter continued her dramatic speech.

"As medical and hospital costs skyrocket," the newswoman was saying, "the number of Registered Nurses working in hospitals is rapidly declining. They claim that hospital management does not understand or appreciate their needs. Nursing school enrollments are down and even experienced veterans like Courtney Quinn here, are leaving the profession in droves. Let's see if we can get a word with her about her unique plan to bring this problem to the public's attention."

Courtney could hardly be considered a "veteran" with only one year of experience under her belt, but then she wasn't exactly a novice either. If the news wanted to call her a veteran, she had no objections. She was just very surprised that she was getting so much free publicity. She decided it must be a very slow day in the news. For once, her timing had been perfect.

"Is it true you're washing your hand of the Nursing profession in order to be a maid?" a reporter was asking of her.

"How has the hospital Administration reacted to your decision to be a maid?" asked another.

"What, if any, offers did management make to keep you in Nursing?" yet another reporter was asking.

Courtney, standing on the step above them, looked over their heads and into the gathering crowd of hospital employees coming to work. She smiled when she saw the face of Paul Edwards in the crowd, beaming up at her and holding his hand up with a "V" for victory sign. She was suddenly relaxed and reassured.

Courtney turned her attention back to the questions of the reporters. Here was her big chance to speak up and be heard. She knew she had to make it count for something and to come across as a professional.

"I have not washed my hands of the Nursing profession," she began. "I simply am trying to draw attention to the fact that nurses are not fairly compensated or appreciated for the tremendous responsibilities that we take. It's true there is a critical shortage of nurses, but it won't get better by sticking our heads in the sand. It's time to speak up about it and to address the problem, before this shortage gets any worse. I want to speak up and see if I can make a difference first."

A round of applause swept through the crowd and Courtney saw Paul give her a thumbs-up sign. She basked in this moment of group approval, suspecting that once she stepped inside the hospital doors, she would be dealing with a lot of disapproval.

By the time she made her way inside, she was almost half an hour late for work. And, though she felt a little guilty, at least she knew that no one would be neglected just because she was late. Her responsibilities were only a fraction of what they used to be. Besides, the publicity was higher on her priority list than getting to work on time was. And speaking of time, where was her time card? She had been told she would be punching a time clock from now on, something that "professionals" didn't have to do. Not that she would have minded. In a way, it would have documented how much of her own time she had given to the hospital for free. No wonder nurses didn't have to punch a clock.

She located her card, punched in, and made her way to the office of her new Supervisor.

"You're late," said a rather stern looking black man who didn't look up from his paperwork.

"I, uh, I'm sorry about that. There were reporters out there and . . . ."

"Yeah, yeah. I know all about it," the man said, disgustedly. "You'll be working with Bertha today. She'll show you what you need to know, then after today you'll be on your own."

The heady feeling from the media attention moments ago was fading. "Which floors will we be covering?" Courtney heard herself ask.

"Fifth and sixth."

"That, uh, that includes 6-South, I guess, doesn't it?"

The Supervisor slowly looked up from his paperwork. "And they say you gotta be smart to be a nurse," he said sarcastically.

Courtney blushed. She hadn't meant to sound so dumb. It was just that it was a little embarrassing to be a nurse one day and a housekeeper the next, on her own floor. She had hoped she would be assigned to any place **but** 6-South. She would bet a week's pay that Alice and/or Steve had something to do with this. But it would take more than this kind of humiliation to make her back down.

"Where do I find Bertha?" she asked politely.

After locating Bertha in the hall outside the office door, Courtney pushed their cart to the elevator with Bertha walking alongside. The cart was equipped with brushes and sponges and disinfectants. They also had several boxes of paper towels and toilet paper. A far cry from the kind of carts Courtney usually pushed, loaded with cardiac monitors, laryngoscopes and cut down trays. The most important piece of equipment, according to Bertha, hung on the handle on the front of the cart. Rubber gloves.

Bertha was just about to show Courtney how to effectively disinfect a bathroom after a patient is discharged, when they were rudely interrupted. A woman dressed in red, and holding a microphone in her hand, approached Courtney as a camera crew gathered around her. The crew was trying to get a shot of Courtney as she began her first day as a housekeeper. The woman in red was shooting questions at her.

"How does it feel to be out from under the responsibilities of being a nurse?" she was asking.

"It feels fine." Courtney tried to answer with a smile.

"Is this what you plan to be doing for the rest of your life?"

A crowd of curious onlookers was beginning to gather. Courtney wanted to be smooth and unruffled and intelligent. All the things she knew she wasn't. She saw Gary peeking out of his doorway, staring at her in astonishment. Saint Jude, help me now, she thought. Send me a witty answer.

"Well, I hope it won't take that long for Administration to realize they have to take our complaints seriously."

Just then, Alice Erickson interrupted the group and told the reporter, on camera, that Courtney had work to do and though she didn't have a specific comment for them at this time, Steve Proctor would be available for comment later this afternoon.

Satisfied, the reporter and her crew left Courtney to get back to work. Bertha handed Courtney a wet mop and pointed her in the direction of Room 657, where a patient had just reportedly spilled a carton of juice.

At first, Courtney didn't recognize the person in the bed. But when

192

finally she did, she gasped. "Maggie Ruggles! What are you doing here?"

"I could ask you the same thing, couldn't I?" Maggie answered, eyeing Courtney's new turquoise uniform.

"I told you I'd do it," Courtney said proudly. "You really didn't believe me, did you?"

"I gotta admit, Quinn, you've got more spunk than I gave you credit for."

"But, really, Maggie," she continued, "what are you doing here?"

"Oh, you know these doctors. Always trying to find something wrong with you."

Maggie went on to tell her that she had gone for her annual employee physical on Friday and had a routine chest X-ray done. The X-ray showed a "suspicious spot" on her lung. The doctor had repeated the X-ray and, again saw the same thing. It was recommended that Maggie be admitted to the hospital for further tests. So far, she'd had lots of tests, but no answers from anyone.

"Anyway, Quinn, why don't you tell me more about this little scheme of yours to get attention," Maggie was saying. "I'm sure it's a lot more interesting than my chest X-ray."

Courtney could hear the apprehension in Maggie's voice, no matter how hard she tried to cover it. But, obviously, Maggie didn't want to talk about it and Courtney didn't know what she could possibly say to comfort this expert nurse. She was only too glad to change the subject.

Courtney told her about the reporters and interviews on the hospital steps this morning. She told her how she didn't want to put up with the conditions of the Nursing Department anymore and that she didn't know how Maggie had put up with it for all of these years.

Maggie shook her head and smiled. "Listen, Quinn. I know your

193

intentions are pure, but you know what?"

"What?"

"You can take yourself out of Nursing, but you can't ever take Nursing out of yourself. It's the nature of the beast. Face it, Quinn. You're doomed to a life of caring."

"What makes you so cynical, Maggie?"

"It's how I survive," Maggie answered truthfully.

"I think you're just afraid," Courtney countered. "I think you're afraid to be happy or to try to make a difference."

Maggie chuckled. "The only thing I'm really afraid of is being a patient. I <u>know</u> what goes on here. I don't want anybody pumping on my chest or cutting holes in my trachea when I go. I hope they just let me go when the time comes."

"Are you afraid of dying?" Courtney asked her bluntly.

Maggie was silent for a moment. The silence was as good as a "yes." She turned her head and gazed out the window. "I'm not afraid of dying," she said. "I figure I paid enough dues on this side of heaven to pay for any mistakes I may have made. That is, if you believe in God and stuff like that."

"Do you, Maggie?" Courtney was intrigued. "Do you believe in 'stuff like that'?"

Maggie was slow to answer. "I got over that stuff a long time ago. If there's a God, then He has a lot of explaining to do. Like, what's the point of having babies born who are only gonna live for a day or two, and torturing them in the Intensive Care Nursery? And why do people have to have pain and suffer the indignities of disease?"

Courtney didn't know what to say. She had never seen this sensitive side of Maggie Ruggles. But Maggie wasn't done yet. She had more to say.

"The way I see it, Quinn, life is just a series of lessons. And just like in school, if you don't learn your lessons well enough, you get left back and repeat the lesson until you've learned it. That's where a lot of people go wrong in romantic relationships. They don't learn the lessons in them." She was silent for a moment, then began again. "Except for you, Quinn. You did pretty well on that one. You're one of the few who learned the first time around with Dave Strauss. You won't repeat that mistake again. I'm glad to see that."

Courtney was surprised. She didn't think Maggie knew about her relationship with Dave. She wondered how many others had known. Courtney didn't want to know. She wanted to change the subject.

"When will the doctors have any news for you?" she asked, sincerely interested.

"Who knows?" Maggie said without emotion.

"I hope you get good news, Maggie," Courtney meant it.

"It's no big deal, Quinn. Like I said, the only hard part is being a patient. In fact, that's probably the only thing that's harder than being a nurse," she laughed.

"Listen, I better get back to work. I don't want to get fired on my first day on the job." Courtney mopped up the spill on the floor and headed toward the door, but Maggie's voice stopped her before she left.

"Quinn, wait a minute."

Courtney turned. "Yes?"

"What you're doing is great. I'm proud of you. I hope I'm around to see the fruits of your labor."

"You will be," Courtney smiled.

195

CHAPTER TWENTY-FIVE

"GIVING FATE A HAND"

The hospital grapevine was humming with a mixture of gossip, facts and rumors. There were two big stories breaking simultaneously. One was about this nurse named Courtney Quinn who had transferred to Housekeeping and whose face was all over the five o'clock news last night. The other story was about another nurse from the same floor who had been found dead in her hospital bed in the wee hours of the morning.

Maggie Ruggles had received some disturbing news that day. The so-called "spot" on her lung was thought to be a germ cell carcinoma, a particularly deadly form of cancer. Maggie Ruggles was no fool. She knew what that meant, and she would have none of it. She refused to sign a surgical consent for a lung biopsy. A team of specialists, some of whom remembered Maggie from their internships, had tried unsuccessfully to talk her into various diagnostic procedures. But Maggie wouldn't hear of it. "If your diagnosis is correct," she had said, "then I'm going to die no matter what you do. And if your diagnosis is incorrect, then I'm going to live to haunt you. In any case, I'm not going to go through chemotherapy or radiation treatments. If I die, I want to die with all my hair."

Rumor had it that Maggie had taken an overdose of barbiturates that she had brought to the hospital with her. Apparently, she had decided that she would have the last word, as usual. It had all happened so fast that it was hard to see the irony at first, that someone like Maggie Ruggles, who had spent most of her adult life taking care of people, now had the problem she feared most. Suddenly she had to really face it herself. It was as though she had been trying to make a deal all of her life, that if she devoted her life to taking care of sick people, maybe she would never have to be sick, herself. The grapevine was saying that anyone who really knew Maggie could have probably predicted her reaction to such a diagnosis. And though she was spared the annoyance of being brought back to life with a million and one tubes in every orifice, she wasn't spared the attempt.

When the Night Nurse made her rounds, Maggie had just looked as though she were sleeping under the dim beam of the nurse's flashlight. The nurse didn't want to disturb her, but when she noticed that Maggie didn't seem to shift her position in bed at all, she became suspicious enough to feel for a pulse. None was there. That's when she called the code. Just about every member of the code team knew Maggie personally. It was the longest code anyone on the team had ever experienced. There were a lot of moist eyes, as Maggie Ruggles finally got her way.

Courtney Quinn was shocked when she overheard the news as she was punching in the next morning. At first she thought she had misunderstood, but the gloom among some of the staff was almost tangible. Everywhere she went, people were talking about what had happened to Maggie Ruggles.

And if they weren't taking about Maggie, then they were talking about Courtney and all the publicity she was getting. The gossip mongers were having a field day.

Courtney was in the middle of stocking the bathrooms with paper towels when the Ward Clerk summoned her to the phone. Who would be calling her now? She assumed it could mean she'd done something wrong already and her Supervisor was calling to tell her about it. On her way to the phone, she wondered if this Housekeeping thing had been a mistake. It was only her second day, but she knew this was not where she belonged. Maybe she had been too gung-ho about taking a stand. After all, in the scheme of things, where did she think this little stunt was going to get her?

"Miss Quinn speaking," she said automatically into the telephone.

"Is this Courtney Quinn?"

The voice was familiar, yet she couldn't place it.

"Speaking."

"Ms. Quinn, how would you like to be on the 'Donald Murphy Show' to talk about your crusade for nurses?"

Of course. Donald Murphy. He was a talk show host on one of Philadelphia's popular T.V. stations. That's how she knew that voice.

"Is this Donald Murphy?" she asked, already knowing the answer.

"It is. So, how's tomorrow? Can you come down to the studio around eight o'clock? We'd like to talk to you while your name is still fresh news."

Courtney was elated. This was more than she'd hoped for. This was her chance to make a difference. To facilitate change in the profession. To speak to a willing audience.

The tide was turning in her favor. She could feel it. And this was only the beginning.

CHAPTER TWENTY-SIX

"SHOCK THERAPY"

Courtney Quinn was a hit on the "Donald Murphy Show." It was mostly because she had done her homework. To begin with, she had asked Donald Murphy for a list of questions he planned to ask her, but he refused. He had said that this was live T.V. and he wanted her answers to be spontaneous.

Courtney then went home and made a list of all the questions she thought he might ask her. She rehearsed her answers until they were smooth and she decided that, if any particular questions stumped her, she would say as little as possible. Rarely had she seen anyone get into trouble for saying too little. Besides, it was Donald Murphy's show and it was his responsibility to keep the conversation going.

Doing her homework had paid off. She had come across as calm and composed, yet there was fire in her eyes when she spoke of the conditions of Nursing that **had** to change and how it was, in the end, the patient who paid for the deplorable shortage of nurses.

Apparently, a lot of people watched the "Donald Murphy Show." Courtney had no sooner arrived home after doing the program when her phone began to ring - non-stop. There were friends and acquaintances congratulating her and others inviting her to come on other talk shows. There were representatives from various Nursing organizations asking her to speak to groups of nurses about her philosophy on Nursing and what she thought each individual nurse could do to cope with the shortage.

It was a heady feeling to be so sought after. Even Dave Strauss called to congratulate her but, of course, he had an ulterior motive.

"What do you say we go out for a little celebration tonight?"

"You and me? Tonight?" A month ago she would have jumped at the chance. She would have told herself that he would change, that he really cared for her. But, nowadays, she knew better. She would not balance herself so precariously on the verge of a broken heart again.

"I don't think so, Dave," she said before she could change her mind.

"Aw, c'mon. You're not still sore at me, are you?"

"I'm not sore, Dave. I just don't want the kind of relationship you're offering me."

"O.K.," he sighed, giving in. "I won't push it right now. But I still think we have a good thing going."

"That's what you say to all the girls." She couldn't help it. She just had to get that little zing in.

"Touché," Dave laughed, not the slightest bit wounded by the dig.

The next phone call was from Alice Erickson, asking Courtney to meet with her that afternoon. This should be good, Courtney thought. She had known Alice wouldn't be pleased with her T.V. appearances, but she had no way to stop her. Or did she? Well, she and Steve Proctor certainly hadn't stopped Courtney from transferring to Housekeeping. So how could they possibly hope to stop her from going on the T.V. talk shows to tell her story and give her opinions.

"I'm afraid I can't meet with you today," Courtney said into the phone, "I'm supposed to work from noon to eight o'clock today."

"I've already taken care of that," Alice said crisply. "I've arranged for you to have the day off."

"But I don't want to lose any pay," Courtney insisted.

"You won't. It's all been taken care of," Alice maintained.

Courtney hung up the phone wondering how an institution that was

200

constantly claiming that they were "over budget" could so easily come up with the money to pay her now for nothing.

When Courtney walked into the now familiar Conference Room in the Administration building, only Alice was there.

"Where's everyone else?" Courtney asked.

"There is no one else. Steve Proctor asked me to meet with you privately."

"It's a lot less threatening," Courtney noted.

Alice began with the usual hospital mumbo-jumbo. But, essentially, what she was asking of Courtney was that she resign from the Housekeeping Department and stay off the T.V. shows.

Courtney laughed out loud. "You don't really expect me to agree to that! What's in it for me? Do you seriously think that I'm just going to go meekly back to Nursing with my tail between my legs and make believe that none of this happened?"

Alice's voice was firm and unwavering. "You're hurting the hospital's public image," she said sternly. "And what hurts the hospital hurts you, since they're the ones who pay your salary."

"I'll take my chances."

"Well, there's one more thing," Alice added cautiously. "Steve Proctor and I discussed it and we're willing to pay you your old Nursing salary while you take a little sabbatical, say for six months or so."

"You're willing to pay me for six months of not working?" Courtney couldn't believe her ears.

"On the condition that you either go back to Nursing or resign from the institution six months from now," Alice added quickly.

"In other words, you're willing to pay me to shut up and drop out of

201

sight," Courtney said, recapping what she had just heard. "Well, I must be having **some** impact if you're that afraid of me appearing on these T.V. shows."

For once Courtney had the upper hand, and it felt good. She knew she must be causing the hospital a lot of embarrassment if Alice and Steve were willing to go this far to keep her quiet. But what about the money? They were always griping that they didn't have enough money to give the nurses a substantial raise. So how was it that they could suddenly afford to pay her a full salary for six months of not working? And, more importantly, **why** were they so willing to do it?

"I'll need your answer today," Alice was saying.

Courtney certainly had no love of her job in Housekeeping, and the T.V. cameras and interviews were taking their toll. But, when all was said and done, she knew she was having an impact on the public's awareness of how shabbily the nurses were treated in this and most other hospitals.

"I can give you your answer right now," Courtney said. "The answer is: Not a chance."

Alice looked disapprovingly at Courtney. "This is the only time we'll be making this offer. If I were you, I'd at least think about it."

"There's nothing to think about. You're trying to bribe me to keep my mouth shut, but it's not going to work. My convictions are not for sale." Courtney and Alice stared each other down for a moment, then Courtney rose to leave.

"Courtney," called Alice.

Courtney turned around, her hand still on the doorknob.

"This conversation should stay between these four walls."

Courtney laughed. "Don't worry, I wasn't planning to tell anyone but the talk show hosts." And with that, she let herself out the door.

Later that evening she was talking to Paul Edwards on the phone. Her relationship with him was so comfortable these days. He not only understood her need to make changes in her profession, he even encouraged and endorsed her methods. It was lovely to have such solid support.

When she told Paul of the meeting with Alice earlier that afternoon and the offer she and Steve had made to Courtney, Paul was more than a little intrigued. He listened carefully to every detail she told him and asked the same questions Courtney had asked herself: Like, where was the money coming from and how could this possibly be fair to the other employees? Paul concluded from their conversation that the hospital Administration was trying to keep a low profile.

Courtney thought nothing more about it. She was just glad she had handled Alice so well today. Paul agreed with her and turned the subject back to planning the next time he could see Courtney - socially.

Courtney slept late into the next morning. She got up and fixed some breakfast and brought it back to bed with her. She turned on the T.V. and curled up on in her comforter, munching on toast and watching the T.V..

She knew she should get up and get dressed for work at noon, but something on the television screen caught her attention. It was the hospital in the background and two people being led out in handcuffs escorted by plainclothes policemen. One of them was Paul Edwards. And she couldn't be sure yet, but from the distant view on the T.V. camera, it looked like it was Alice Erickson he was escorting. Yes. Yes it was! And the other person being led out was Steve Proctor. The T.V. news reporter was saying something about corruption and embezzlement.

Courtney was shocked at first, but as the shock wore off, she couldn't stop laughing. Steve Proctor and Alice Erickson had been in cahoots and were embezzling money from the Hospital! Courtney heard Paul being interviewed by the news reporter. He was telling her that he had been working undercover on this case for some time now. He had posed as a plainclothes policeman who was supposedly guarding cops and police informants who were also patients. But he had really been there to unravel the embezzlement. No wonder he had listened so carefully to her recounting her conversation with Alice last night! And no wonder Alice had offered her money to be quiet and get out of the spotlight.

A lot of things made sense now.

Epilogue

It was a full house at St. Jude's Roman Catholic Church for the wedding. And, though it was the middle of January in Philadelphia, the mood was festive. Pink and white balloons were anchored with pink ribbons to the church doors and played touch-tag with each other in the winter wind. There was a spotlight on the front of the church so that photographers and onlookers could get a good look at the bride as she entered the church for the evening wedding. Someone had even strung soft pink light bulbs through the branches of the bare trees outside the front door and candles burned in the windows of the little chapel. The church was filled with well-dressed and delighted wedding guests.

From the choir loft, a blonde-haired man with sad blue eyes stared glumly down at the crowd and wondered what he was doing there. How could she have asked him to be the organist at her wedding? Sure, he had talent, and sure, he was an accomplished musician, among other things. But the fact was, he was still in love with her. Maybe he wasn't very good about saying it or showing it, but she **had** to know he still felt it. Didn't she?

He thought about how beautiful she would be today. If only she could have waited just a little longer. He would have asked her to marry him - eventually. He'd just needed his freedom and a little more time to be certain before making a commitment like that. Who could blame him for playing the field? But it was too late now. In just a few minutes, Courtney Quinn would float down that aisle on her father's arm, and pledge her love and her life to someone else.

Big decisions had always been difficult for David Strauss. Courtney knew that. She should have given him more time. After all, he was only thirty-five! He didn't see any reason to rush into anything. Sadly, he sank down onto the wooden bench in front of the organ and began to play softly. At least the last words he would say to her would be musical ones.

The atmosphere was thick with low murmurings except for a group of thirtyish looking women on the bride's side who were animated in their conversation.

"I can't wait to see her," said the one. "She's going to be a beautiful bride."

"I can't believe Courtney is getting married. I mean, it's such a traditional thing to do and we both know she's not the traditional type. She's always been such a rebel."

"I know. Plus she's always had such terrible luck with men," said the first one again. "Can you believe she has that schmuck, Dave Strauss, up there playing the organ?"

"Well, can you blame her?" piped up another of the women. "She certainly played his organ long enough. I think it's poetic justice."

The group of women burst into laughter together and heads turned to see what could be so funny in a wedding chapel.

A few pews closer to the altar, some sixtyish women in fox jackets and too much makeup conferred.

"Well, I thought I'd never see this day. Thank God she decided to stop running around and settle down. The only thing is, I wonder why she didn't find herself a nice doctor to marry?"

"I heard she was going with one fella who was a doctor. I don't know what happened to that, though. She should have hung onto him, if you ask me. She's still gonna have to put up with late night emergency phone calls if she marries a cop."

Just then, a teenaged boy walked slowly up the side aisle, genuflected in front of the altar, then moved to the side and knelt before the statue of Saint Jude. He lit a candle in front of his favorite saint, and bowed his head.

A man in one of the front pews nudged his wife and nodded toward Gary Evans. "Isn't that the kid who was a patient of hers? You know,

206

the one they said had an inoperable brain tumor?"

"Oh, yes," answered the wife. "I think so. I'd heard he was going to be here."

"It's been about six months now, they say, since his miracle cure. I heard Courtney talking about it. She said there's not even a trace of the tumor to be found."

"God is good," murmured the wife, eyes staring straight ahead.

Standing in the back of the church was a rather attractive red-headed woman, accompanied by a young man in a wheelchair. The man held her hand in both of his and every now and then the diamond on her finger would glimmer under the antique chandeliers. She looked lovingly at the man and smiled.

"I hope they'll be as happy as we are," she said, her face glowing with love for the man in the wheelchair.

"I'm sure they will be," he replied as he pressed the woman's hand to his lips. "Courtney Edwards," the man said. "I like it. It has a nice ring to it."

The woman smiled knowingly. "I'm glad you like it, but her name is going to stay 'Courtney Quinn.'"

"Why doesn't that surprise me?" laughed the man. "Anybody who worked as hard as she has to make a name for herself shouldn't change it, I guess."

"She's worked hard, all right. At first, I didn't think I agreed with her tactics, like transferring to Housekeeping, but look where it got her," Karen Beal beamed at her husband.

"Yeah, she set out to make a difference in Nursing and she sure made an impact around here. Do you think she'll ever go back to just plain Nursing?" her husband asked.

207

"I don't think so. Not in the sense that you mean, like working in a hospital. She's already booked on a couple of T.V. shows on the West Coast and all kinds of Nursing organizations have been calling her and asking her to speak to their groups. She's going to be a very busy lady."

"But she'll always be a nurse," Karen's husband teased. "You nurses are devoted. You'll always have it in you."

Just then, the organ music stopped, and five bridesmaids assembled as the congregation rose in unison to the familiar strains of the "Wedding March" filling the tiny chapel.

Look-alike bridesmaids filed down the aisle, eyes straight ahead, bouquets slightly trembling. And then, there she was, all smiles and radiance, the picture of tranquillity on her father's arm. She floated up the aisle turning her head from side to side to smile and greet friends and relatives. Everyone later remarked on her calmness, her smoothness, her serenity.

The beaming Paul Edwards took her hand as she reached the altar and, forgetting himself and the well-rehearsed ceremony, kissed her full on the lips. A ripple of laughter spread through the church and, Father Quinn, the bride's uncle, quipped, "Well, what else can you expect from two people who handle emergencies all the time?"

"You look so calm and beautiful," Paul whispered to his bride.

She looked up at her new almost-husband's face and beamed. "I think I'm going to be incontinent," she said.

GLOSSARY

ACT OF CONTRITION: Catholic prayer in which the sinner admits to his/her wrongdoing, asks forgiveness, and resolves, with God's help, to avoid wrongdoings in the future.

ADMISSION: A person coming into the hospital as a patient. Usually arrives at the worst possible time or fifteen minutes before the nurse gets off duty.

AIR MATTRESS: Inflatable plastic mattress, sometimes resembling an egg crate, used to prevent bedsores.

AMBU BAG: Rubber bag with mask that fits over the patient's nose and mouth or trachea and forces air into the lungs when squeezed; first thing to grab when a patient codes as it eliminates the need for mouth-to-mouth resuscitation.

ATELECTASIS: Incomplete expansion of lungs.

BAGGING: Forcing air into the lungs of a person who cannot breathe on his/her own. This is done by squeezing a hand-held ambu bag. As in, "The patient was 'bagged' during the code."

BUNIONECTOMY: Removal of a painful bump on or near the big toe. As in, "Yes, I know we only did a bunionectomy and osteotomy, but your third toe fell off any way."

CAROTID PULSE: Palpable beat of a major artery that runs through the neck and supplies the head with blood. Also, the first thing to look for if you suspect a patient is dead.

CHANGE OF SHIFT REPORT: Meeting of off-going and on-coming nurses, where each patient's orders and progress are reviewed. Also, a signal for patients, visitors and doctors to come out of comas, ask for bedpans and pain medication and write "stat" orders.

CHEMOTHERAPY: Use of chemical substances in treating disease. As in, "The patient puked his guts out after chemotherapy."

CODE: A set procedure for resuscitating a patient with cardiac or respiratory arrest. The act of using a set procedure to resuscitate a patient. As in, "Send me some more help, my patient is coding."

CODE CHIEF: The person running or directing the code; usually a medical resident, but sometimes just the doctor who barks the loudest.

COUMADIN: An anticoagulant agent, used to prevent pulmonary embolism. As in, "I think we've been giving the patient the wrong dose of Coumadin."

C.P.R.: Cardiopulmonary resuscitation. As in, "He's not breathing. Begin C.P.R."

CRAP TRAP: Invention by Maggie Ruggles, R.N., to avoid the fuss and bother of multiple incontinent patients. A thick tube attached to a disposable drainage bag is inserted into the rectum of any patient who is bedridden or incontinent.

D AND C: Dilation and Curettage. Also known as a "Dusting and Cleaning."

D.N.R.: Do Not Resuscitate. As in, "Leave me alone when I die. Make me a D.N.R."

DECUBITUS ULCER: Bed sore. As in, "Those new air mattresses Alice Erickson bought actually **CAUSE** decubitus ulcers."

DIRTY UTILITY ROOM: A room, usually in the vicinity of the Nurses' Station, where specimens from bedpans are collected and/or measured. Also where dirty linen is thrown and where bedpans are emptied. Also, an excellent place to have a conversation since no one goes in there unless they absolutely **HAVE** to.

E.K.G.: Electrocardiogram

E.R.: Emergency Room

EMESIS: Polite way of saying "Puke."

EPSTEIN-BARR: The virus known to cause mononucleosis.

EPSTEIN'S BARR: Tavern owned by Sam Epstein, where hospital workers go to unwind.

FACE SHEET: First page of a patient's chart; contains vital information about the patient. As in, "Look on the face sheet to see what kind of insurance the patient has."

F.L.E.A.S.: Medical residents. Term is partially derived from the number of medical interns and residents who surround a dying patient likes fleas on animal excrement. Stands for, "Fucking Little Egotistical Assholes."

FLOAT: Taking a nurse or a nurses' aide from her area of expertise and putting her in a completely unfamiliar environment, usually due to sick calls. As in, "Float a nurse from Orthopedics to Intensive Care Nursery."

G.O.R.K.: A diagnosis for patients who have no particular diagnosis, but who are not communicating or responding well enough to suit hospital personnel. Stands for "God Only Really Knows."

HEPARIN: Injectable drug used to "thin" the blood and to treat existing blood clots as well as to prevent new ones.

HEPARINIZE: To inject and maintain a patient with the therapeutic dose of Heparin.

HIP PINNING: Surgical fixation of a fractured hip.

HYPER AL: Short term for a thick solution of highly concentrated nutrients, usually given intravenously. Also, a nickname for a medical resident named Al, who hyperventilates.

I.C.U.: Intensive Care Unit

INCIDENT REPORT: Form, made out in triplicate, describing an unusual event or series of events. Usually filled out by nurses after a medication error, or a patient falls out of bed. As in, "Administration says the Incident Report is for our own protection, but nurses say it is used as evidence to get them fired."

I.V.: Intravenous

I.V. NURSE: Registered Nurse who carries a black bag and goes all through the hospital drawing blood and starting I.V.s. Also known as "The Vampire."

JULY FIRST: The first day the medical students turn into interns and interns turn into residents. Also the day that smart nurses and informed patients stay away from the hospital.

LAPAROTOMY: Surgical incision into the abdomen.

LEECH THERAPY: A means of treating venous congestion, usually in the fingers, by attaching a blood-sucking, worm-like creature called a leech.

LEUKEMIA: A type of cancer of the blood which causes proliferation of abnormal cells.

LUPUS ERYTHEMATOSUS: A degenerative disease of the connective tissue, characterized by skin inflammation.

M.A.O. INHIBITOR DIET: Stands for monoamine oxidase inhibitor diet. Patients taking certain medications, usually a particular type of antidepressant, must avoid foods such as cheese, chocolate and wine because they contain monoamine oxidase and can cause serious side effects when combined with certain drugs. Has nothing to do with "mayo"nnaise.

M.V.A.: Motor vehicle accident.

MALIGNANT SCHWANOMA: A tumor of the nerve fibers.

METASTASIS: The spread of disease from one part of the body to another.

NECROTIC: Death of a piece of tissue that has been injured. "I think the toe we operated on is necrotic now."

N.P.O.: Abbreviation of Latin term for "nothing by mouth."

NURSES' AIDE: Person who takes a six to twelve week training course to assist patients under the direction of a nurse.

NURSE RECRUITER: A Registered Nurse who receives full salary (plus trips overseas) to lure nurses into working at the hospital she represents.

NURSES' LOUNGE: A misnomer. A room usually used for writing frantic notes on charts or for housing overflow patients for the night.

NURSE'S NOTES Documentation of a patient's condition required to be written by a nurse every two hours. As in, "My shift was finished over an hour ago and I still have all my Nurse's Notes to write."

O.R.: Operating Room

O.R. GREENS: Scrub clothes used by hospital personnel who work in a sterile area. Also worn in Epstein's Barr to impress non-hospital personnel.

ON-CALL ROOM: Room usually in separate part of hospital where "on-call" personnel sleep . . . or play.

ORTHOPOD: Orthopedic Surgeon. Considered by some to be strong as an ox, and twice as smart.

OSTEOTOMY: A surgical procedure where a bone is divided or a piece of bone is removed.

P.T.A. BATHS: Type of bath given to patients when the ward is more short staffed than usual. Stands for "Pits, Tits, and Ass." Also known as "A lick and a promise."

PARANOID SCHIZOPHRENIA: A psychotic disorder characterized by loss of mental contact with reality and delusions or hallucinations.

PARAPLEGIC: A person whose lower half of the body is paralyzed.

POST-OP: A patient who has recently had surgery. As in, "I can't take another admission. I have sixteen fresh post-ops."

PRAYER FOR VOCATIONS: A Catholic prayer asking God to call a person to the religious life.

PRIAPISM: An abnormal and often painful erection of the penis, which is not due to sexual desire.

PULMONARY EMBOLISM: Obstruction of a blood vessel of the lung by a blood clot that usually has been broken off from the deep veins in the leg.

QUADRIPLEGIC: A person who is paralyzed in all four limbs.

RADIAL PULSE: Palpable beat of a large artery near the radius or wrist bone. As in, "The housekeeper says she doesn't have a radial pulse."

RADIATION TREATMENTS: Treatment for destroying cancer cells with energy in the form of waves.

RALES: The sound (usually heard through a stethoscope) of air passing through congested or mucus-clogged part of the lung.

REQUIEM: A Catholic Mass for the repose of the dead.

S.O.B.: Short of Breath or Son of a Bitch, whichever applies.

SICKLE CELL ANEMIA: A blood disorder, usually among people of African descent, characterized by crescent shaped red blood cells.

SKELETAL TRACTION: A type of traction that is applied by inserting a pin through a bone and applying weight to it.

SPHYGMOMANOMETER: A blood pressure machine, sometimes on wheels. At least one of the wheels malfunctions at all times.

SPUTUM: Polite way of saying "spit."

STANDARD DISCHARGE ORDERS: Procedures routinely carried out the night before a patient is discharged. Procedures are done in order to prevent anything from happening (like running a fever or falling out of bed) that might postpone the impending discharge. Orders include: (l) Two aspirin or acetaminophen every four hours to prevent fever, (2) pillows on the floor surrounding the bed, and (3) deliberately withholding news of impending discharge from the patient.

STAT: Drop everything, this is important. As in, "Get me a cup of coffee, stat."

STOOL: A small, four legged step for reaching high places. Also a polite word for human excrement.

SUBCLAVIAN LINE: An I.V. placed into a large vein just beneath the collar bone.

T-SPINE: Thoracic spine; the part of the spine that enters into the formation of the thorax or chest.

T-12: The twelfth vertebra in the thoracic spine. As in, "The bullet severed the spinal cord at the T-l2 level."

THREATENED ABORTION: A possible loss of the fetus during the first twenty weeks of pregnancy, characterized by abdominal cramps and a slight show of blood.

TELEPHONE ROUNDS: Technique of gathering information regarding patients' conditions and workload of nurses, via telephone. Used by doctors and Nursing Supervisors alike to avoid facing overworked and frustrated nurses.

URINAL: A cylindrical container used by male patients to urinate in. So far, no one has come up with a suitable version of it for female patients. Also, can be used as a vase when visitors bring flowers.

VALIUM: A medication used for short term relief of anxiety. As in, "Give me a Valium, I'm being floated tonight."

VARICOSE VEINS: Abnormally dilated and swollen veins, usually in the leg. As in, "I have to get out of Nursing before my varicose veins and bunions get any worse."

VENOUS THROMBOSIS: The presence of a blood clot within a vein.

VITAL SIGNS: A person's body temperature, pulse and respiratory rates and blood pressure. As in, "The patient is going downhill, but his vital signs are stable." Or, "The presence or absence of the crash cart is a vital sign of how busy the ward will be on the next shift."

ABOUT THE AUTHOR

Joan Brady, R.N., B.S.N., is a graduate of William Paterson College, Wayne, New Jersey. She has over twenty years of varied nursing experience including staff nurse, head nurse, specialty nursing, and per diem. For the past several years, Joan has been a "Traveling Nurse." This experience has taken her to many parts of the country and has offered her a unique opportunity to see and experience first hand the universal problems facing the nursing profession.

Joan has published articles, contributed chapters for nursing text books and appeared on radio and television. Her appearances have focused primarily on the topic of Nursing Burn Out. She has also taught courses on burn out and other topics of interest to nurses.

Joan's creative writing talent, her humor and insight will inspire nurses and, will tell our story to those who are (or one day may be) our patients.